Reconsidering Christianity

An Expedition of Faith
Joining Science, Ancient Wisdom,
and Sustainability

RON RUDE

[RE]CONSIDERING CHRISTIANITY © copyright 2012 by
Ron Rude. All rights reserved. No part of this book may be
reproduced in any form whatsoever, by photography or xerography
or by any other means, by broadcast or transmission, by translation
into any kind of language, nor by recording electronically or
otherwise, without permission in writing from the author, except
by a reviewer, who may quote brief passages in critical
articles or reviews.

ISBN 13: 978-1-59298-547-0

Library of Congress Catalog Number: 2012915092

Printed in the United States of America

First Printing: 2012
Printed on 30% recycled paper

16 15 14 13 12   5 4 3 2 1

Cover and interior design by James Monroe Design, LLC.

BEAVER'S
POND
PRESS

Beaver's Pond Press, Inc.
7108 Ohms Lane, Suite 101
Edina, MN 55439–2129
(952) 829-8818
www.BeaversPondPress.com

To order, visit www.BeaversPondBooks.com
or www.abel-emerging.com
or call (800) 901-3480. Reseller discounts available.

To my campus ministry students,
for their inspiration and energy.

Contents

Introduction

As a child, I attended church with my family and remember numerous Sundays listening to the pastor's sermon. Although I don't recall much of what he said, my clearest memories have to do with questions whose answers, to a little boy, were quite baffling; namely, why would anyone want a job like that? Who would choose such an occupation? How can he possibly come up with a sermon each week?

Well, here I am today, a pastor. Perspectives change as we age. Oddly enough, preaching and teaching are actually what I enjoy most about this life work. For more than thirty years, I have been engaged in this and other tasks as an ordained minister in the Evangelical Lutheran Church in America (ELCA), and I currently serve as Lutheran campus pastor at the University of Arizona in Tucson.

We should expect changes in perspective and worldview as time passes. Life is its own teacher. My current congregation consists of college students, and I do my best to plant the idea that the university years are a time to grow away from one's Sunday school faith toward a college-level faith, and hopefully from there into adulthood. Why? Because childhood beliefs don't generally work in college; and our perceptions as young adults probably won't meet our deepening needs as we mature.

It's difficult to identify precisely when and where my own specific changes—my own transformations—occurred. I do know, however, that a number of significant convictions that I held deeply in earlier years no longer hold sway today. I believe differently now than I did then.

It can be scary when we discover that something of former significance is no longer sufficient. One solution is to retreat. People seem to be able to find numerous ways to recoil from life's challenges. Another option is to discipline oneself to refrain from questioning certain sacred fundamentals. Indeed, some Christians vigorously warn fellow believers not to give space or standing to those disquieting (re)considerations that bubble up in the soul from time to time. After all, some say, it just might be the devil messing with you. However, for me, it is actually the adventure of faith that draws me to these questions. It is in faith that I plunge into the arena of rethinking, reconsidering, and reframing Christianity's "version(s)" of God's story of life and God's story of Jesus.[1]

For me, leaving home and going to college was an adventure of its own, an adventure into the humanities. Initially majoring in music—I wanted to be a high school band director—

---

1.   I use the word "version" intentionally. God's story of life and God's story of Jesus consists of what "is." Only the Creator knows this story, since such complete knowledge is far beyond the purview of any created creature, including humans. So in the absence of what actually happened, we possess versions. A version is just that; an estimation, an approximation, a version. It does not equal the actual. So the Bible is an assortment of versions of God's story of life and God's story of Jesus. So is historic Christianity, so are the sciences, and so are art, literature, and film. All of these versions have much to teach. However, as important as they are, and although some approximations are much closer to reality than are others, we should embrace them with studied humility for what they are and what they are not.

I later switched my focus when the call to seminary began to tug. My new major was what my school called a distributive major, which was basically five minors—history, philosophy, psychology, religion, and music—sewn together. My academic advisor at the time wisely surmised that a background in the human condition would provide helpful context for both biblical/theological study in seminary and parish ministry afterward. So I explored the humanities and continue to do so today. I particularly enjoy world history, politics, biography, the arts, and American history, especially approached through the autobiographies and biographies of the U.S. presidents.

However, about seventeen years ago, my interests took a new turn. I became intrigued by the so-called "hard" or natural sciences. While living in Buffalo, New York, from 1985 to 1996, the beguiling geology of the Niagara escarpment, the stunning Finger Lakes region, and the runneling legacy of Earth's most recent glacial period captivated my imagination. Later, when in Denver, Colorado, from 1996 to 2001, I was surprised to learn that the Rocky Mountain system before me, with its peaks, valleys, rivers, and basins, is actually the *fourth* such mountain formation to have arisen and eroded since Earth's early beginnings. Driven up by massive molten forces deep beneath the Earth's crust, this latest manifestation of metamorphic and sedimentary rock began surging skyward approximately 70 million years prior to the invention of Twitter.[2]

My curiosity has only broadened since moving to Tucson,

---

2. Earth's solid iron inner core is so compressed and so hot that iron and nickel metals around it become a liquid molten outer core. Surrounding this outer core is a layer of rock (not quite solid and not quite molten) called the mantle. As this mantle extends farther away from the searing center, it cools, eventually cooling sufficiently to produce a hardened crust. This hardened rock crust (similar to a layer of skin on a cooling bowl of oatmeal) ranges in thickness from three miles at the bottom of the world's deepest ocean trenches to sixty-one miles under some continents. Beneath the Colorado Rockies, the crust averages thirty miles in thickness.

Arizona, in 2001 and working in a university setting. I find exploring the beautiful Sonoran Desert ecosystem with its mountains and arroyos, cacti and animal wildlife endlessly fascinating. I take a hike every morning before breakfast and usually see coyotes, antelope jack rabbits, mule deer, various desert birds, numerous desert plants, javelina, and, if I'm lucky, a reclusive bobcat. My interests also include geology, evolutionary biology, astronomy, and horticulture, the latter of which I am exploring through organic vegetable gardening, composting, and rain-water harvesting. I'm definitely a layperson in all these fields, and I don't pretend to be otherwise. I have tremendous respect for people who engage in research and teach in the various natural sciences. But what little I have come to understand as an eager amateur has proved transformative to my previous worldviews and beliefs.

I have always found it wise to let fields like history, literature, psychology, philosophy, language, music, and other such humanities influence my understanding and practice of the Christian faith. But now astronomy, geology, evolutionary biology, and ecology beckon as well. And I realize my former belief systems no longer satisfy. After fishing on one side of the boat for most of my life and catching relatively little of significance, I find that the natural sciences (as well as other life experiences) are coaxing my nets into deeper waters on the other side of the vessel. As a result, my theological nets are so full of fish that they are on the verge of tearing! And this is exciting.[3]

My first book, *Abel Emerging: A Reconsideration of the Christian Story for a Sustainable World* (Beaver's Pond Press, 2010, **www.abel-emerging.com**) laid the narrative groundwork for this "shaking of the foundations."[4] Since its publication, I

---

3. The disciples of Jesus had a similar experience in Galilee centuries ago when their worldviews were altered. See John 21:1–11 and Luke 5:1–11.

4. *Shaking of the Foundations* is the title of an out-of-print book by the great German theologian, Paul Tillich (New York: Charles Scribner's Sons, 1955).

have spoken to community and church groups, interacted with readers, continued my research, and harvested wisdom from many sources. *(Re)considering Christianity* further explores and maps the intriguing implications of what for me is a reconsidered, reframed, and recast telling of the greatest story ever told.

Many readers will find the seminal ideas in this book not only challenging, but also unsettling—at least initially. If you are one such reader, I can only encourage you to persevere to the end. It may take a while for my proposals to sink in—as my wife continues to remind me. Although what you read may likely be somewhat different from what you have considered previously, my hope is that it will ring true and feel familiar to your soul at some level. Perhaps reading one chapter every day or two will set a nice pace if you find the ideas challenging or new.

Before beginning, let me say a word about footnotes; you will discover them at the bottom of many pages. I invite you to see them not simply as necessary citations or tedious distractions, but rather as treasures. They will send you on excursions into many side topics that are connected to the story of life. And you might be enriched by what you explore.

There are three appendices. The first presents my view of biblical interpretation. The second introduces a gifted singer-songwriter named Annemarie Russell (**www.annemarierussell.com**), who writes and performs in music what I am trying to convey in prose. The third appendix contains a thoughtful sermon by my daughter, Jen. Jen is a Lutheran (ELCA) pastor in Chicago who displays a creative way of looking at old biblical stories. Finally, at the back, there is an annotated bibliography. The books listed there have educated me greatly and helped me put into words what had stirred deep inside.

Each of us is an "expeditionary" in this life. We are travelers bound to God's creation, searching for meaning. This is certainly true of those who would call themselves Christian. Christianity itself is a *movement*. A disciple is one who *responds* when Jesus says, "*Follow* me" (John 1:43, emphasis added). Apostles are those who are *sent*. "As the Father has *sent* me, so I send you" (John 20:21, emphasis added). As his final instruction, Jesus commanded "*Go* and make disciples of all peoples" (Matthew 28:19, emphasis added), and, "you shall be my witnesses in Jerusalem, in all Judea and Samaria, and to the ends of the earth" (Acts 1:8b). We do not learn the truths of life and faith by remaining stationary. The act of discovery, and then that of figuring out what to do with what we find, entails stepping out onto the road of life and into the fields and furrows on the side of the road. "*Go* and learn what this means," Jesus counsels to ensure that we have the life experiences necessary to help us grasp what he is teaching (Matthew 9:13, emphasis added). The truths that we will find in the journey of life reside alongside rolling fields of green corn, thunderclaps echoing down a valley, the seasonal migrations of both birds and peoples, and nature's impulses, both at the morning sunrise and in the final moments before death. They reside at the center of life and abide in the margins, amidst the neighing of horses, the excited babblings of children, and the silence, or plaintive cry, of hunger.

Fullness of life and the depths of truth summon those with a heart to be an adventurer, an explorer, an expeditionary. This may be the first time you are giving serious consideration to God's story of life and God's story of Jesus. Or, after long years of living within the Christian community, you may have come to a time when you are *re*considering these things. Either way, my hope is that my expedition of faith joining science, ancient wisdom, and sustainability will inspire you and your community in the journey you travel, now and tomorrow.

—*Ron Rude*
www.abel-emerging.com

PART I

God's Primary Mission:
The Evolving Story of Life

Forget not the rhythm nor the dance
That echoes deep and holds you fast
Forget not the soil that nurtures with plan
The tree of life, Creator's hand

—Annemarie Russell, from "Around Me"

Chapter 1
Vast and Ancient

We start our journey of seeing God's story of life by looking through the lens of astronomy.

On a clear, dark, and moonless night, if one is lucky enough to reside sufficiently distant from the pollution of city lights,[5] one can see the nocturnal sky littered with stars from the galaxy in which we reside: the Milky Way. Planet Earth, a "Goldilocks planet," spins on its axis in one insignificant arm of this vast

---

5.   In the 1970s, the city of Tucson, Arizona, made the decision to restrict human-caused light pollution. Primarily for the benefit of the high-level telescopes at Kitt Peak forty miles to the southwest, which divulge some of the best views of outer space that can be found anywhere on the planet, Tucson residents wanted to keep their nighttime skies as dark and pristine as possible. So the city devised standards/rules/laws designed to inhibit outdoor light emissions in every facet of commercial, municipal, and residential life. As far as I know, almost every thoughtful Tucsonan cherishes these restrictions on visual blight and none feel deprived.

collection of stars.[6] We orbit one of its stars—we call it the Sun—traveling through space at a speed of 67,000 mph. While we grace one star with the name "Sun," every other star in the sky is actually some kind of sun, too. Most of these sun/stars have their own solar systems, with their own orbiting planets, as astronomers are discovering each day. Therefore, what we really see in the starlit night are thousands and millions of suns.

The nearest star and solar system to our own is called *Proxima Centauri*. It resides 4.2 light years away from my door-step on the west side of Tucson. With this distance of 4.2 light years, light photons traveling at the speed of light—186,282 miles per second, or 670 million miles per hour, or 5.8 trillion miles per year—will require approximately four years and two months to travel the twenty-four trillion mile distance from *Proxima Centauri* to Earth. Needless to say, 24,000,000,000,000 miles is an enormous distance.

These two stars, our Sun and *Proxima Centauri,* are not the only stars in our Milky Way galaxy, however. There are approximately two hundred billion others. These expand even further into space for trillions of additional miles. And if that's not mind-boggling enough, the Milky Way, with its 200 billion stars, is just one galaxy out of approximately 210 billion others in the known universe. These stretch almost endlessly into outer space. Some of these galactic marvels contain as few as one hundred thousand suns/solar systems and others more than three trillion (3,000,000,000,000).[7]

Although astronomers are pretty certain that the basic

---

6. The term "Goldilocks" refers to Earth being the right size (7,926 miles in diameter) and right distance (93 million miles) from the sun—not too close or far away, not too hot or cold—so as to be able to sustain life as we know it. Earth also has a dense atmosphere to protect us from excessive ultraviolet radiation, and an abundance of water which serves as a basic solvent for the chemistry of life.

7. It wasn't until the 1920s that astronomers found evidence of other galaxies beyond the Milky Way.

elements necessary for life exist throughout the universe—even the elements that make up our own solar system, including Earth, came from exploding supernova in faraway reaches—it is unlikely that significant contact will ever be made, given these extreme distances. Nevertheless, theoretically, life extends throughout the vastness of space.

Not only is God's universe incredibly vast, it is also ancient. I don't use "ancient" here as one might when speaking about ancient Rome, ancient Mesopotamia, or even ancient China. These civilizations are newborns by science's standards, since their existence began only a few thousand years ago. God's universe, on the other hand, is at least 13.7 billion years old. Our Sun and Earth are about 4.6 billion years old, and the miracle of life has existed on planet Earth for about 3.7 billion years. (See figure 1 on page 12 for a helpful timeline of the universe.)

Figure 1: General Timeline of the Universe

2,000 years ago	Christianity begins
3,500	emergence of Israel
7,000	writing invented
8,000	Cain's culture
12,000	new forms of agriculture and animal domestication
14,000	Great Lakes form
35,000	Neanderthals die out; only *Homo sapiens* continue
40,000	evidence of cave paintings, figurines, bone carvings, burial of dead
70,000	modern *Homo sapiens sapiens*
120,000	Neanderthal *Homo sapiens*
200,000	*Homo sapiens* (Abel)
400,000	first evidence of constructed shelters
780,000	*Homo erectus* migration out of Africa
790,000	evidence of domesticated fire in hearths of predecessor hominids
1,900,000	bison in North America
2,500,000	predecessor hominid species use tools to hunt, prepare food, construct shelter
2,600,000	23 successive cycles of ice ages begin, making lakes and rivers
4,000,000	predecessor hominid species (*Australopithecus, Homo habilis, Homo erectus*)
5,500,000	formation of Grand Canyon begins
20,000,000	primates appear
35,000,000	felines appear
50,000,000	some land mammals evolve back into ocean (whale, dolphin, manatee)
65,000,000	mammal surge after dinosaur extinction
125,000,000	marsupials (kangaroos and koalas)
140,000,000	fruit-bearing plants
195,000,000	mammals
200,000,000	super-continent Pangaea begins to break apart
295,000,000	reptiles (including dinosaurs)
320,000,000	insects first take flight
395,000,000	sea life moves onto land
425,000,000	trilobites, brachiopods, cephalopods, reef systems

Timeline of the Universe Continued . . .

543,000,000	Cambrian explosion: burst of life diversity
660,000,000	multiple-celled life emerges (some scientists say 1.2 billion years ago)
1,300,000,000	cellular reproduction
1,750,000,000	single-cell life (eukaryotes, cells with nuclei)
2,300,000,000	oxygen increase from algae
2,700,000,000	photosynthesis
3,700,000,000	single-cell life (prokaryotes, cells without nuclei)
4,500,000,000	Sun and planet Earth
13,700,000,000	universe begins

It is difficult to wrap our minds around such staggering datings and figures. But again, we can turn to the speed of light—186,000 miles per second—to provide perspective. Light emitting from the Sun, for example, at the speed of light, takes approximately eight minutes to travel to Earth. That's a distance of ninety-three million miles in eight minutes. What does this mean to you and me? It means that if a person steps outside at noon today and looks (with safety eyewear) at the Sun, she won't be seeing the Sun's appearance at that moment, but rather how it looked at 11:52 a.m., that is, eight minutes earlier.

Similarly, when we look at our neighboring star/sun *Proxima Centauri,* we are seeing what this star looked like four years and two months ago. As we noted earlier, this is how long it took the image we see today to travel the twenty-four trillion miles to our eyes. Similarly again, our nearest neighboring galaxy outside the Milky Way resides 2.5 million light years into the distance. This means that the image we will see tonight through our telescopes actually commenced its inter-galactic journey to Earth when nature pushed the "send" button 2.5 million years before the final episode of *The Oprah Show.*

As we might imagine, such remarkable numbers and staggering distances prompt many fascinating questions. One such question is this: Does gazing into the heavens allow us to peer back in time, to see the past? The answer is yes. In fact, astronomers have seen light images coming from galaxies more than thirteen billion light years away. We don't even know if these primitive configurations exist today, although astronomers are pretty sure they do not. But we do know that these stars existed thirteen billion years prior to our day. And we can determine, based on what we observe through sophisticated telescopes, what they looked like back *then*.

So not only is God's universe unbelievably vast, it is also exceedingly old. It seems that "God the Father Almighty," whom Christians and others acknowledge as the "maker of heaven and Earth" and the one whose reign permeates "all that is, seen and unseen," has been engaged in this creativity business across a large expanse of expanding space for a long, long time.[8]

---

8.   In the year 1654, Archbishop James Ussher of Ireland "determined" that biblical calculations set Earth's age at six thousand years. He even asserted an exact date for the genesis of everything, 23 October 4004 BCE, which some camps within Christianity still ascribe to today. In the mid-1700s, a Scottish geologist named James Hutton began to understand that minerals in granite were once molten, and that erosive forces over long periods of time created sedimentary rock. He thought the Earth was eternal, "no vestige of a beginning, no prospect of an end." In 1862 William Thomson started understanding the processes of heat energy and deemed the Earth's age to be between twenty million and forty million years old. In the early 1900s New Zealand-born physicist Ernest Rutherford began to understand radiation. He calculated Earth's age at around five hundred million years old. Since then, science has learned even more, and today a consensus of scientists from many fields have established Earth's beginning at around 4.5 billion years ago. This information can be found in numerous geology books.

Chapter 2
Eden Was Good, Not Perfect

The Bible has a few things to say about this cosmic and ancient story of life. In the Genesis 1 creation story (dated around 500 BCE), the storytellers portray a creator who not only makes the whole universe vast and varied, but makes it "good." "And God saw that it was good" (Genesis 1:12). The Hebrew word for good is *tov. Tov* is a rich and multi-layered word that describes a world about which the Creator is very pleased (see also Genesis 1:4, 10, 18, 21, 25, and 31).

It is important to remember that, contrary to popular notions, the word *tov* does not mean "perfection" or even "paradise." Such understandings are actually Greco-Roman constructs that arose at a much later time in history, well after the Genesis stories were written down, and were imposed backward onto this earlier Hebrew narrative. In the Hebrew way of thinking, the world that God intentionally made, Eden, was good (*tov*), not perfect; and this is an excellent thing.

So what is included when we say that God created a good universe, especially as it relates to our planet and the approximately twenty million species, including us, who reside and evolve here? A *tov* Earth includes many things. It includes wind, rain, seasons, fungi, and earthquakes. Earthquakes? Yes. Apparently the Creator made our planet with earthquakes. Why? Because without them, Earth would probably be dead; no life could exist. Earthquakes are actually part of a colossal circulation system interweaving the elements of a Sun-energized biosphere with the elements of molten mantle deep beneath the Earth's crust, circulating and recirculating everything up and down, over and over again. Such a grand system of moving currents is required for a planet to be alive, at least as scientists understand life processes at this time. Plate tectonic movements appear to be helpful and maybe even necessary for the emergence and sustenance of life.[9]

Tov also includes termites, snow and ice, uplift and erosion, and lightning. Lightning contributes to the nitrogen cycle in the soil that nourishes plants, as well as the water cycle that generates rain. It may be part of what sustains life. If lightning hits my or my neighbor's house, we will obviously consider it a bad and unfortunate thing. Certainly, no one wants this to happen. But for the whole and health of God's larger creation, lightning appears to be good and essential.[10]

---

9. Earth's seven major and many more minor tectonic plates of crust material are constantly moving (or floating) at a rate of one to four inches per year over the hot rock of the upper mantle. When these shiftings build up enough pressure and then snap, this is an earthquake (or tremor).

10. Benjamin Franklin (1706–1790) invented the lightning rod in the 1750s. This simple instrument diminished the terror of fires and electrocutions caused by lightning strikes. Oddly enough, as Franklin's discovery caught on, some religious people criticized him for messing with God's "message delivery system." They reasoned that a struck barn, house, or business meant God was displeased, and the owners had better shape up.

Tov includes photosynthesis, reproduction, chemical reactions, and hurricanes. Hurricanes not only distribute the accumulated hot air around the equator belt to other parts of the globe, a necessary process for planetary well-being, they also help cross-pollinate vegetation, insects, reptiles, birds, and other animal life between atolls, islands, and continents. Again, if a hurricane hits me or mine, it is a terrible thing—from our perspective. But on the grander scale, hurricanes are part of God's *tov* garden of life.

Tov includes evaporation, conductivity, forest fires, and bacteria. Bacteria species are essential to the story of life, facilitating such processes as oxygen creation, mineralization, nitrogen and sulfate cycles, fermentation, and the purification of wastewater. Billions of these tiny organisms even live inside our human bodies, as well as on our skin. We are very dependent on them for our survival. In fact, without bacteria, life on Earth, including human life, would come to a stop. These microorganisms also carry diseases such as leprosy, tuberculosis, diphtheria, and tetanus. But in the larger picture, bacteria are part of God's *tov*. Joel Salatin, third-generation family farmer at Polyface Farm in Virginia's Shenandoah Valley, writes,

> Life is not sterile. Biology is not sterile. Things that won't rot, or won't decompose, or a disposal system that impairs decomposition, all characterize inanimate things, mechanical things. We are surrounded, inside and outside, with bacteria and decomposition. The entire principle of recycling hinges on the ability of something to decompose. Leaves, grass, carcasses of bugs and animals. Trees that fall over. The life, death, decomposition, regeneration cycle is both physically and ecologically fundamental and profoundly spiritual.[11]

---

11.   Joel Salatin, *Folks, This Ain't Normal*, 113.

There is also balance. If the birthrate of lions soars, then an excess of antelope gets eaten and the antelope population decreases. This will soon cause starvation among some of the lions until balance asserts itself again. If the antelope birthrate soars, the increase in food supply will allow for more lions to be born, which then grow up to eat more antelopes until the antelope population goes down enough to restore balance. This balancing act of life and death occurs simultaneously on hundreds of thousands of levels and stages. Along with this, there is a food chain, or food network. All species get their nourishment from consuming other species. Noting such patterns in the natural world, Richard Heinberg writes,

> At first ecologists studied food chains—big fish eating little fish. Quickly they realized that since big fish die and are subsequently eaten by scavengers and microbes that are then eaten by still other organisms, it is more appropriate to speak of food cycles or webs. Further analysis yielded the insight that all of nature is continually engaged in the cycling and recycling of energy and matter. There are carbon cycles, nitrogen cycles, phosphorus cycles, sulfur cycles, and water cycles.[12]

The list is endless, really—volcanoes, conductivity, sex, youth, middle age, old age, viruses, life, and death. In the eyes of the biblical storytellers, God has made the world *tov*. And *tov* is not only good enough, it is very good in God's eyes. "God saw everything that was made, and behold it was good, very good" (Genesis 1:31).

---

12.   Richard Heinberg, *The Party's Over*, 15.

So what about the inclusion of death in the previous paragraph? Is this part of God's *tov* garden of life, too? A positive answer may seem strange to some, but consider how odd the world would be if there were no death and dying, if everything that had been birthed just persevered forever. What would the planet be like? We think it is crowded now. Think how many Gila wood-peckers there would be, and beluga whales, Chilean mesquite trees, and dinosaurs. How about woolly mammoths, Canadian geese, salamanders, and *Homo sapiens*? Such a scenario is too bizarre even to contemplate. For good reason the Creator has woven death into the fabric of life. Life and death and death and life are allied in the Creator's house, this *tov* biosphere with its many and varied dwelling places. This cycle allows for life to be replenished. Furthermore, as an aside, knowing that our life is terminal can help us cherish the short time we do have to live.

We can use many adjectives to describe the amazing richness of God's garden, and probably all of them will be inadequate. This world is remarkable, and the more we learn about it, the more spectacular and complex it becomes. But God's garden was never meant to be perfection, a paradise, or even utopia. In fact, "utopia" (from the Greek: *ou-topos*) literally means "no place." "No place," by definition, has never existed, not in the recent or distant past, not today, and not in the future. Rather than a utopia, God's garden is alive, and is ever evolving on a multitude of levels. It is *tov*.

Chapter 3
Humanity's Recent Arrival

How do humans fit into the community of life? This is a question about which we are rightly curious. Actually, our appearance is relatively recent when we put it into perspective. According to cosmologists, physicists, astronomers, and geologists, as mentioned earlier, the evolving universe began some 13.7 billion years ago, with the Sun and planet Earth forming about 4.6 billion years ago. Physics existed from the universe's beginning moments, with chemistry following soon thereafter.

Approximately 3.7 billion years ago, the processes of chemistry on planet Earth began to evolve into another marvel called biology. That is, nonlife became life. Single celled at first, it would take another three billion years for these emergent, tiny creatures to figure out how to cooperate enough to become multiple-celled creatures. That this transition took such a tremendously long time is an indication to scientists of the magnitude of this grand leap.[13]

Roughly 395 million years before Abner Doubleday purportedly invented the game of baseball in 1839, Earth's atmospheric oxygen (O_2) approached current levels, as sea life began moving onto land—first plants, then insects, and eventually vertebrates. Reptiles, including dinosaurs, appeared around 295 million years ago, with mammals coming about 100 million years later. Those mammals remained rather small until the dinosaurs disappeared (except for those that evolved into today's birds) 65 million years ago. This massive extinction created new evolutionary spaces, or niches, which resulted in mammals being able to grow larger.[14]

And a fascinating side note: approximately 50 million years ago some of those land mammals began evolving *back* into the sea, probably in search of food. Hence, some mammals live in the ocean. It turns out that whales, dolphins, porpoises, manatees, dugongs, sea lions, seals, and sea otters not only share unique bone structures and other physical characteristics with land elephants, cows, wolves, felines, and weasels, but also remarkably common DNA. Though some whale mammals can hold their breath for up to an hour, they and all other aquatic mammals must eventually come to the surface to breathe air

---

13.   Other major innovations noted by biologists include the chromosome, bounded cells, meiosis and sex, the eukaryotic cell, gastrulation, mulluscan torsion, and segmentation. These were watershed events in the explosion of evolving life.

14.   The extinction of dinosaurs, which occurred 65 million years ago (MYA), is one of five mass extinctions in Earth's geological history. The others took place 465 MYA, 370 MYA, 251 MYA, and 225 MYA. When the dinosaurs disappeared, half of all known species disappeared with them. The major accepted theory for this sudden destruction involves the effects of a 10 km Chicxulub meteorite crashing along Mexico's Yucatan peninsula with an impact of 10^{14} tons of TNT. This cataclysm caused massive earthquakes and sent clouds of debris into the skies, blocking sunlight, rearranging the biosphere, and wiping out the food systems on which dinosaurs and other large creatures depended.

into their lungs.

Primates have been around for more than 20 million years, separating into our branch of origination about 7 million years ago and eventually into our immediate predecessor species such as *Australopithecus, Homo habilis,* and *Homo erectus* about 3 to 4 million years before our time. For at least 800,000 years and maybe for as long as 2 million, some of these ancestors harnessed fire for heating, cooking, and protection. From these forerunners derived our own species, *Homo sapiens,* which appears to have been present about 200,000 years ago, with a more modern version called *Homo sapiens sapiens* dispersing around the globe for the past 70,000 years. Although both were anatomically similar to ourselves, the emergence of *Homo sapiens sapiens* refers to the remarkable transition within our species from intuitive, non-symbolic, and nonlinguistic ways of processing and communicating information to the more language based and symbolic mental manipulation of information and ideas that we enjoy today.[15] (Again, see figure 1 on page 12 for a visual of these dates.)

These numbers can be hard to keep straight. And though they are widely accepted by scientists in a variety of disciplines, they should be considered with humility. But even when allowing for generous margins of error, it is still striking that the Creator's house, with its many dwelling places, has

---

15.   This summary is admittedly oversimplified. For a more extensive look, see Ian Tattersall's book *Masters of the Planet: The Search for our Human Origins.* New York: Palgrave MacMillan, 2012. The author is curator of the Hall of Human Origins at New York's American Museum of Natural History. Although I would argue that the first half of the title is inflated, it is nevertheless a brilliant examination of current palaeoanthropology.

been around for a long, long time.[16] And while it is true that the species *Homo sapiens* is in its infancy, other species are even more nascent, having appeared subsequent to our arrival.

Two creation stories in the Hebrew scriptures offer insight into the nature of our species. These are found in Genesis 1, which has already been mentioned, and Genesis 2. Genesis 2 is actually the older narrative, written around 900 BCE. In this parable the storytellers portray humans, represented by Adam (in Hebrew: *adám)*, as creatures composed of soil, earth, and dirt (in Hebrew: *adamáh)*. Note the similarity of the Hebrew words, *adám* and *adamáh*. Human beings, according to the storytellers, are earthlings. Or better, dirtlings. We are created from the soil and are made alive as Yahweh "breathes into their nostrils the breath of life" (Genesis 2:7).

It is not possible for biblical scholars to know precisely what these storytellers meant in using these images. However, it is striking to observe the similarities between their insight into the earthiness of our species and current understandings in the field of evolutionary biology. As a simple microscope can begin to show, one square foot of soil is teaming with billions of life forms, including bacterial decomposers, microbes that attract atmospheric nitrogen into the soil to feed plants, mites, fungi that foster plant immunity, earthworms, and insects. As these creatures live, so we live. Perhaps an understanding of humanity that seeks to remove or cut off our species from inti-mate connectedness with the rest of creation (our "family of origin" in family systems thinking) would not only be against the storytellers' implied understandings, but might also produce significant neurosis. As one farmer put it, "The further

16. See John 14:1-7. I understand the Creator's house to be wherever the "reign of God" exists. For Christians this includes not only heaven but also the whole universe, including Earth. The reign of God (or kingdom of God) is a way of talking about God's permeating presence and ownership, the acknowledgement of which is eminently important to Christians.

humans get away from the soil, the crazier they become!"[17]

Genesis 1 is also instructive. Even though it is located prior to Genesis 2 in the Bible, it was actually written several hundred years later, around 500 BCE. Genesis 1 is filled with beautiful liturgical/poetic imagery concerning the proper observance of the Sabbath, all carefully placed within the framework of the number seven (as in seven days). The number seven in the Hebrew scriptures signifies wholeness and completeness. One of the striking things about this passage is the language it employs during the creation of the human creature. In Genesis 1:26–27 the storytellers write, "And God said, 'Let *us* make humankind in *our* image'" (emphasis added). This occurs on the sixth day in the sequence of events and comes after God's creation of "the wild animals . . . the cattle . . . and everything that creeps upon the earth" (Genesis 1:25). Interpreters have long pondered the meaning of such curious phraseology. To whom is God talking? Who are "us" and "our"? Is it a heavenly host of some kind? Could these pronouns refer to the Trinity (obviously not a Hebrew or Jewish interpretation)? Is this a literary device known as the "royal we"? These are commonly accepted views and consistent with what I learned in seminary.

But perhaps the storytellers had something else in mind. When the Creator says, "Let us make humans in our image," perhaps God is addressing not the Divinity (or Godhead) itself, multiple or singular, but rather the other Earth life-forms already on the scene, that is, the fish and ocean reefs, insects and forests, plants and animals. Might the storytellers be sharing the view that humans are intended to mirror both the image of God *and* the image of all the other evolving creatures in God's garden of life—and that we forget either at our

---

17. Christianity at its best has tried to maintain this connection. For example, the funeral liturgy of many traditions refers to the soil as the source of life while we live, and our destination when we die. "Earth to earth, ashes to ashes, dust to dust."

peril? "Let *us* [God and animals together] create humankind in *our* [God and animals together] image." Again, biblical scholars can only speculate as to the biblical writers' actual aim. And certainly, in the spirit of a concept known as Occam's razor, the standard and simpler interpretation, that is, that humans are uniquely created in the image of God, is easier to digest. Nevertheless, such a close biological and visceral bond between our species and Earth's other varied life-forms is quite consistent with the findings of evolutionary biology, making the wider interpretation at least intriguing.[18]

The members of species *Homo sapiens* display a diverse assortment of features, capabilities, and quirks. Some among us are able to compose music, while others design and erect tall buildings. Some excel in the culinary arts, while others solve complex mathematical problems. Intelligence varies within our species, as do physical prowess, imagination, artistic abilities, sexual and gender identities, and longevity, among other characteristics. But like all other creatures, our own particular

---

18.   Scholars have noted significant differences between the two creation stories in Genesis. These variations become part of the data for determining their dating.

- In Genesis 2 the Deity is called Yahweh (an earlier name for God). In Genesis 1, it is the later name Elohim.
- In Genesis 2 the Deity creates physically, that is, "formed the *adám* from the dust of the ground" (2:7a), "breathed into his nostrils the breath of life" (2:7b), "planted a garden" (2:8), "made to grow" (2:9), "out of the ground the Lord God formed every animal" (2:19a), "brought them to the man" (2:19b), "took one of his ribs and closed up its place with flesh" (2:21). And later, "they heard the sound of the Lord God walking in the garden" (3:8). These acts of creation were all very physical. In contrast, the Deity in Genesis 1 creates and behaves orally, that is, by simply speaking: "And God said 'let there be . . . and there was'" (Genesis 1:3, 6, 9, 14, 20, 24, and 26).
- In the Genesis 2 parable, a male member of *Homo sapiens* is created first, followed by trees and vegetation (Genesis 2:4–5, 7–9), animals (Genesis 2:18–19), and finally the female member of the species *Homo sapiens* as the consummation. In contrast, in the Genesis chapter 1 story, the creation of both female and male members of *Homo sapiens* occurs together at the end as God's final, wrapping-up activity on the sixth day.

combinations of abilities and disabilities have proved sufficient.

That said, it is also worth noting that we are quite under-developed in many areas, when compared to other life forms. For example,

- We cannot fly at all, let alone fly backward and upside down like a hummingbird.

- We are clumsy on our feet compared to a mountain goat or mule.

- We have terrible hand-eye coordination compared to that of a squirrel.

- In terms of speed, we rank in the middle: faster than walruses (on land) and slower than cheetahs.

- Our eyesight is four times less sharp than that of an eagle, and our olfactory (nose) sense is a million times less sensitive than a common bloodhound.

- We cannot change color like a chameleon, Arctic fox, or tree toad.

- We cannot store water like a desert tortoise, Fishhook barrel cactus, or Bactrian camel (which can go up to ten months without drinking water).

Nevertheless, the Creator has supplied us with ample gifts and capacities consistent with living responsibly with and within the community of life. Equipped with abilities such as reason, symbolic thinking, and language, among other things, our species has been able to thrive, educate ourselves, and migrate throughout the globe.[19]

So far, we have looked briefly at the vastness and age of God's story of evolving life. And we have begun to consider what science and the biblical narratives together imply about the human species in this enormous and lengthy saga. (Again, see figure 1 on page 12.) As we embark on the task of (re)considering Christianity, several questions arise. First, if God's story of life is so ancient, why are Israel and Christianity so recent? These cultures/religions have been around for only 3,500 years and 2,000 years, respectively. Second, why is the predominant and pulsating message of both the Old and New Testaments the "reign of God" (also translated the "kingdom of God" or "realm of God")? Is this reign of God intended to contrast the reign of someone or something else? And third, why are we, that is, why is the species *Homo sapiens*, the addressees in these recent narratives?

---

19. Scientists from various disciplines have traced global human migration. First emerging in Africa 200,000 years ago, humans began spreading in waves into the Fertile Crescent and southern Asia 80,000 years ago, into southern Europe and the Iberian Peninsula 60,000, 40,000, and 10,000 years ago, into Australasia and the Oceania Islands 65,000, 30,000, and 10,000 years ago, into China 40,000 years ago, and into the Americas perhaps as early as 25,000 years ago. Migration is tracked by examining bone fossils, gene pool markers (mitochondrial genome for females; Y chromosomes for males), archeological evidence, sedimentary deposit layers, linguistic/language analysis, tool comparisons, and even the spread of certain diseases that only humans carry such as *hepatitis* 6, bacterium pathogens like *helicobacter pylori* (common in stomach ulcers), and even lice.

What follows are responses to these questions.[20]

---

20. At this point the reader may wonder about my approach to biblical interpretation. What is this collection of sixty-six books? Why are there so many different literary forms such as letters, genealogies, laws, poetry, wisdom sayings, historical accounts, myth, parables, and more? What parts can be understood clearly and what parts not? What do we do with what we discover in the Bible when we find it, and how do such findings relate to other venues of knowledge such as science, the arts, life experience, archeology, reason, and intuition? What if Christians disagree among themselves? Are there many right ways to look at a passage, or only one? See appendix A for a brief discussion on the process of Biblical Interpretation.

PART II

A Species Gone Awry

*"When one tugs at a single thing in nature,
he finds it attached to the rest of the world."*

—John Muir

Chapter 4
The Fall: More Recent than Original

I do not know the definitive answers to the questions I posed at the end of chapter 3. These questions, and my uncertainty, have puzzled me and others for some time. However, I have a theory. This theory is inspired in part by the writings of Daniel Quinn (**www.ishmael.org**) and Raine Eisler (*The Chalice and the Blade: Our History, Our Future*), as well as other readings in the social sciences and theology. Let me sketch it here.

Recently, perhaps 5,000, or 7,000, or 9,000 years ago, a paradigm shift began occurring among a few of the many thousands of human cultures spread around the planet. This shift had to do with an alteration in self-perception, a revision of thinking, a change in worldviews. The notion of paradigm shift has been posited in recent years. The idea suggests that occasionally unpredictable events occur that effect monumental changes in the world. In our time, we can think of the Holocaust, the fall of the Soviet Union, or the election of Nelson Mandela as president in South Africa. Who could have forecast such unanticipated occurrences? Other eras of human history have brought the emergence of speech into our species, the domestication of agriculture and animals, a switch from Roman numerals to Arabic numerals which enabled higher mathematics, the realization by Europeans of the American continents, and the discovery of germ theory. In geological time, there have been high-impact glacial periods, massive movements of continents, and climatic changes that affected whole swathes of planetary existence. And in terms of the whole universe, at some point, nothing became something, nonlife became life, and the incredible mystery of consciousness appeared. These substantial shifts are unwieldy in their complexity and often impossible to document. However, what appears certain is that something that was before is no longer as it was, and something new is now the pattern.

So what was this shift about? What had changed? The gist of this shift—this new way of thinking, according to the theory—was this: the species *Homo sapiens* is to be considered "special." We are special in the eyes of the Creator. We are special in relation to all other natural forces and life-forms. In fact, we are *more* special and important than all other natural forces and life-forms *put together*.

The people of these cultures likely embraced this new ideology unconsciously at the start. Furthermore, it didn't show up in any one moment or even over the course of several centuries, but came on slowly and subtly over numerous generations. After living in a relatively compatible manner with and within the community of life for approximately 200,000 years—something that must have been true in order for *Homo sapiens* to have continued evolving[21]—recently, a few cultures of our species began to change directions. Out of the tens of thousands of human cultures dwelling in Earth's mountains and forests, deserts and tundra, along riverbanks and coastlines, upon plains and prairies, a handful of peopled cultures began roaming down a different pathway.

As this new philosophical, and later theological, worldview/narrative/myth began to take hold, according to the theory, these few human cultures began to function differently than they had in prior eras. They began to function as though humans were separate *from* the rest of the universe, superior *to* the rest of the universe, the reason *for* the rest of the universe, and the rulers *of* the rest of the universe. They began to think of themselves as greater than the rest of the community of life on Earth, and as occupying center stage, with everything else basically revolving around, and created primarily for, them. Some

---

21. Contrary to popular understanding, the notion of evolution is not so much "survival of the fittest" as it is survival of those species that "fit in." Charles Darwin (1809–1882) did not use the phrase "survival of the fittest" in his 1859 *The Origin of the Species*. Rather, an English contemporary named Herbert Spencer (1820–1903) coined this phrase and transferred it into the realm of human economic and military "struggle for existence." This became known by the misnomer "social Darwinism."

Also, for many people the notion of evolving life implies "progress." However, the idea of progress is debatable even among evolutionary biologists. Although a species certainly evolves in order to keep fitting in with a changing world, such change does not necessarily mean progress, or things getting better. Is a penguin today "better" than a penguin 10 million years ago? Is a birch tree more advanced than an ancestor birch tree 10,000 years ago? Are humans today superior to their forebears? We are different, certainly, but has there been progress? For example, if I were to exchange places with a human being from 50,000 years ago, which of us would learn more quickly how to survive in the other's world?

Finally, while competition for resources is an important factor in evolution, as is procreation, scientists in recent years have been giving more attention to the vital role of cooperation in evolutionary processes.

humans began to think of themselves as primary.[22]

The bottom line of this new way of thinking was this: humans rule. This worldview in some circles has become known as human exceptionalism. According to this viewpoint, humans should consider themselves exceptionally exceptional, that is, standing apart from everything else. Others have referred to it as anthropo-centricism (human-centeredness). A friend of mine calls it "diva" theology.

Over a short period of a few thousand years, this radically new worldview not only emerged, but began to spread, taking root in some cultures but not in others. The Greek philosopher Protagoras (485–410 BCE) captured this wave by declaring: "Man is the measure of all things." Humans are the yardstick, the plum line, and the standard by which everything else ought be judged and valued. The seventeenth-century philosopher Francis Bacon (1561–1626) described it for his time and culture: "Man, if we look to final causes, may be regarded as the center of the world, insomuch that if man were taken away from the world, the rest would seem to be all astray, without aim or purpose."[23] In both of these quotations the message is clear—it's all about us. The time is fulfilled, the kingdom (reign) of humans is at hand; submit, adapt to us, or get out of the way.

Over the past 5,000 to 9,000 years, more and more cultures

---

22. We have self-designated ourselves "primates," which means "primary." Some even presume we are the most primary of primates—the head of the class, the front of the line, the top of the toppest. We also have appraised ourselves the name *Homo sapiens, sapiens,* which means "wise, wise one." One wonders if other creatures, or even the Creator, concur with this self-assessment.

23. Benjamin Kline, *First Alone the River,* 9.

have adapted this new worldview of human exceptionalism.[24] During these relatively recent centuries, this new worldview has deepened and spread and ascended to where it is today *the* dominant and domineering narrative of almost every culture of our species, including our own. Indeed, a major paradigm shift has occurred. Today, this narrative has become so common that it saturates our text books and term papers, our television programs and commercials. It is the inspiration of many a graduation speech, the unchallenged "given" of both civil and uncivil discourse, and the underpinning of so much in daily affairs. It propels myriad actions, from industrial farming to fracking shale for oil. It pervades politics, philosophy, newscasts, warfare, and talk radio. It is the air we breathe and the airwaves that incessantly engage, teach, entertain, and eventually numb us. It is barely noticed but ever-present. It has even usurped and domesticated Christian theology, in my view. Certainly many preachers and theologians will feign "the world belongs to God." But the oft underlying presumption and understanding is that providentially and obviously, "God gave it to us."

This worldview of dominion has taken many forms over the centuries. For some it translates into forthright exploitation and abuse, like the "Christian" preacher I heard on the radio

---

24. I realize that it is nearly impossible to determine the worldviews of early humans prior to this suggested paradigm shift. According to palaeoanthropologist Ian Tattersall in *Masters of the Planet: The Search for our Human Origins*, verbal language in our species arose about 70,000 years ago, with oral traditions perhaps emerging in due course thereafter. There are a few scarce samples of ancient art that are suggestive of how some people thought, but it is only with the recent invention of writing, about 7,000 years ago, that we begin to have actual evidence. We know almost nothing about the 200,000 years of *Homo sapiens* history prior to the written word. Does this mean ancient peoples had insignificant lives and worldviews? No. It just means that we don't know them. However, what I am suggesting, but admittedly without evidence for or against, is that early peoples lived more "in relationship" with the world around them than we do today. This has certainly been witnessed in some indigenous peoples and so-called "primitive" cultures around the world. What I am suggesting will become clearer as we proceed.

one Sunday morning who claimed that God intended humans to treat the Earth much like a paper towel—we are to use it up and throw it away. To do otherwise is to suggest idolatry—to be worshipping and serving the creature rather than the Creator—he supposed. And it's all passing away anyway, according to this thinking. Others, including some in my own religious tradition, have argued that God put humans in charge, but gave the Earth to humans in order for us to care for, protect, and improve on it. We are to be earnest stewards, not abusers, of God's precious gift. However, either way, the underlying assumption is essentially the same: the Earth (some even think outer space) is primarily for and about human beings. Humanity is God's primary obsession, and humanity's temporal administration and ultimate welfare is God's foremost, if not sole, concern. Even those few Christians who value the care of the Earth and creation stewardship, and those fewer still who actually practice it, frame it in such a way that "we are preserving the environment for future (human) generations."[25]

As these few cultures of humans began to flex their muscle in the direction of this newfound narrative, the principal effect was that members of these cultures grew more and more out-of-relationship in a number of specific ways. They grew out of relationship with

- their human neighbors

- creation

- their own inner spirit/souls/selves

- the Creator

---

25. Given the vastness and age of God's story of life, it seems to be an overstatement to assert that humans are the reason for the story, or that the community of life needs our stewardship. Life has survived and thrived for eons without our interference, let alone presence. It will continue to do so long after we are gone. With this in mind, perhaps it is more accurate to say that the world does not need humans to steward the world, but rather the world would like our species to self-regulate and steward *ourselves*.

As they grew distant from their human *neighbors,* they were ever more inclined toward suspicion, violence, and breach. Conflicts escalated, and interdependency diminished.[26]

As they disconnected from God's *creation,* they began thinking of the wider community of life—the soil, water, air, plant and animal life—as an "it," a thing, a mere commodity. Soon, they came to regard God's garden of life as a jungle: a dangerous, deficient, defiant, disorderly enemy. It was wild and needed to be tamed, broken and needed to be fixed, inept at self-rule and needed to be conquered. It was a wasteland in need of "development."

They lost sight of their own *inner spirit/souls/selves.* While snubbing inner contentment, they became addicted to wanting more and more props, to chasing one new spectacle after another, to craving the novel, fantastical, bizarre, or simply "whatever it is I don't presently possess."

And they regressed into a state of estrangement from the center and circumference of all that was, is, and will be: God the *Creator.* Members of these few cultures became creatures who were at odds with the world and with God. They more and more dwelled in a state of disconnectedness, restlessness, and "existential disrepair." And their worldviews and behaviors produced such disquieting effects so as to leave much of the community of life, including their own species, "groaning in travail" (Romans 8:22).[27]

---

26. It's important not to idealize or romanticize humanity's behaviors prior to these changes. There has always been and will always be conflict as various groups rub up against one another. Groups and species are always partial to the "home team." What I am suggesting here, and in the paragraphs to come, is an enormous shift in scale.

27. In his wonderful book *Manna and Mercy,* Daniel Erlander writes, "Humans decided to find joy in becoming big deals. How did humans know if they were big deals? They knew by bossing others around, by piling up stuff, by dominating nature, and by reaching glorious heights of health and beauty and knowledge. They also knew by having more points than others in their scoring systems" (p. 2).

The author Daniel Quinn (**www.ishmael.org**) presents a fascinating thesis about this shift in thinking and behavior, and how it relates to the Bible. He proposes that the biblical stories of Adam and Eve in the *tov* garden of Eden (Genesis 2–4), as well as the stories of Abel and Cain (Genesis 4), Noah and the flood (Genesis 6–9), and the tower of Babel (Genesis 11) were written as responses to this shift happening among some peoples of their world. In other words, the storytellers of Genesis created parables/myths to address actual historical circumstances occurring in their time and locale, circumstances that they observed and experienced.

What this means, according to Quinn, is that the stories of Adam and Eve were not meant to describe two actual people living on the Earth six days into the history of the universe. Furthermore, Quinn suggests that they were not two actual people who, through their disobedience toward God, triggered not only the lethal infection of sin that was to ever after affect all of humanity, but also an infection of sin and brokenness that was to affect the cosmos itself. This literal view of Adam and Eve is held by a portion of Jews and Christians in various camps and persuasions, though not generally in my own tradition.[28]

But according to Quinn, neither were Adam and Eve primarily symbolic. They were not meant to serve as metaphors for what is timelessly considered by the storytellers to

---

28. Very few biblical scholars, theologians, seminary professors, bishops, or pastors in the ELCA Lutheran community or other Christian communities such as United Methodist, Presbyterian, American Baptist, Episcopalian, United Church of Christ, and even most Roman Catholic consider Adam and Eve to be actual, historical persons. In other words, the human species did not begin with two unbirthed first parents (did they have belly buttons?) who populated the Earth by having sexual intercourse with each other and producing children, who in turn had sexual intercourse with their siblings and nieces and nephews and cousins and in-laws and so on.

   Furthermore, there were not two actual people named Adam and Eve whose bad behavior brought natural calamities such as hurricanes, disease, earthquakes, and death into a formerly perfect paradise. Such a view would argue that the actions of Adam and Eve not only altered the fate of humanity, but also the fate of the cosmos. That is, both humanity and the creation "fell."

be amiss in human nature. They were not, for example, representations of all humans throughout history, including our time, who disobey God's commands, deflect responsibility, hide when guilty, blame others when caught, and play God. We certainly do these things, no doubt, but this is not what these stories were about.

Rather—and this is Quinn's intriguing insight—these stories were meant to be specific to the time (3,000 to 4,000 years ago) and locale (the Middle East) of the storytellers. These writings were attempts to understand, name, contextualize, and put into parable form troubling changes in actual historical circumstances witnessed in the storytellers' specific communities. Sea-change shifts in thinking were infiltrating their homes from neighboring regions of the globe. Alternative worldviews, haughty self-understandings, and boorish behaviors that had originally emerged only in isolated portions of the human community a few thousand years earlier—a blink of an eye, really—were now arriving at the storytellers' doorstep. These new worldviews were gaining traction. They were spreading a disintegration of well-being. And they were producing toxic forms of denigration throughout their local community.

This suggests that, in the realm of Christian theology, there *may* be something called "original sin." However, this is not what these Genesis stories are about according to Quinn. Rather, these "Fall" stories in Genesis 3 and following address something else, something more perverse, something happening much closer to our own time. They address real events occurring far into the human era, in the storytellers' locale and time, some 70,000 years after we emerged as modern *Homo sapiens*.

As the storytellers observed the behavior of these intruders into their time and place, they wondered, what's wrong with these people? Why do they behave this way? Why do they champion discordance, not only against other humans but also against God's creation? Why do they exhibit a disquieting

I-centeredness? Do they think they are extraordinary? Do they presume that the world revolves around them?

Devising parables to articulate these puzzling observations, the storytellers imagined that these people had perhaps trespassed God's domain, an event they symbolized as involving a tree of the knowledge of good and evil. Perhaps they had stepped over the line of demarcation and differentiation between Creator and creature, by "eating fruit" not only forbidden by any save Yahweh, but also fruit terrifyingly perilous in the wrong hands. Like a two-year-old performing brain surgery, a three-year-old trying to summit Mount Everest, or a mere military general being given the authority to obey orders from a mere politician to deploy and launch weapons of mass destruction, they were in over their heads. In eating this fruit, they had encroached on an authority entirely beyond their physical, ethical, intellectual, technological, and spiritual aptitude. Having eaten, they presumed to have digested what the fruit embodied, namely wisdom, and now regarded themselves as a species "like God" (Genesis 3:5).

Another way to say this, using a different metaphor, is to describe these strange people as having absented themselves from the Creator's household under the permeating reign of God, and instead as having declared their own house under the dominating and domineering reign of humans. With themselves at the center, they deemed the world their own.

In the prequel to this book, *Abel Emerging: A Reconsideration of the Christian Story for a Sustainable World*, I employ the Abel and Cain story (Genesis 4) as a background literary template for this theory. "Abel" cultures are those cultures that live under the permeating reign of God with and within the whole community of life. They are "Leaver" cultures (Daniel Quinn's term) in that they "take what is needed and leave the rest." They are neither perfect nor inferior, saints nor devils, savages nor "noble" savages. However, they are generally in an interdependent relationship—with neighbor, with God's creation, with their inner spirit/souls/selves, and with the Creator. Therefore, they are very much favored by the Creator, not so much for their offerings, but for the way they acquired their offerings (Genesis 4:4–6). Having such natural relationships makes all the difference to their behavior as a species, rendering their quirks, foibles, and even sins manageable.[29]

"Cain" cultures, on the other hand, are those in which humans position themselves beyond everything else—separate from, superior to, the reason for, and the rulers of the Earth. They generally live out of relationship with their neighbors, isolated from the Creation, cut off from their inner spirits, and detached from the Creator—even though they may be very religious in their rhetoric and rituals. In Cain cultures, intelligence is measured by the ability to control mystery and reduce it to technology. Military power and economic wealth together combine to leverage the world in Cain's favor, to feed Cain's militaristic, acquisitive, "entitlement" consumerism.[30] In short, Cain is a "Taker" (another Daniel Quinn term) who takes and takes, and then takes more.

---

29. Again, it is important not to romanticize Abel and Leaverism. Such living did at times embody destructive religions practices, detrimental gender and marriage rules, warfare and conquest, and even thoughtless harm towards the soil, air, water, and plant and animal life.

30. Walter Brueggemann first introduced me to this concept. It describes a worldview that declares my right to consume all that I want, provided I am able to pay for it. If certain resources, such as oil, minerals, land, a cheap work force, are in another nation and I have the money to buy them, I am entitled to those resources. In fact, if anyone tries to deny me those resources, I have a right to use economic, political, or military warfare to get them. Further, if humanity's desires are at odds with the well-being of the wider community of life, humanity's entitlement takes precedence. Hence, the term "entitlement consumerism."

According to Cain's narrative, the garden was made for humans, so humans must conquer it. We must use it as desired and discard the rest as expendable. To serve humans is the reason for the garden's existence; this is the purpose for which it was created. Furthermore, we should not cease our quest to command land, sea, sky, weather, plant and animal life, bacteria, genes, etc., until humanity's holy mission is fulfilled and all creation lies bleeding at our feet, until we have transformed both God and nature into the image of humans. Cain believes that not only should his culture behave imperially toward other human cultures around the planet, but also that the human species itself should behave in empire-like fashion toward all the other life-forms in God's community of life.

To think of people and cultures as either Abels or Cains provides a helpful way to distinguish two very opposing narratives. These narratives produce two dramatically different ways of living and being in God's world.

As the Cain narrative took hold, the biblical writers continued to record their observations in parable form. In Genesis 6:6, in what may be the saddest verse in the Bible, the storytellers wrote, "And God was sorry that he had made the human creature, and it grieved him to his heart." After nurturing life on Earth for 3.7 billion years and the species *Homo sapiens* for 200,000 years, including modern *Homo sapiens* for 70,000 years, God faced a terrible problem: a wayward species was on the loose. Humans were spoiling the *tov* garden of life. They were behaving in homicidal ways, with the real possibility of becoming eventually and ultimately suicidal.

What was the Creator to do? This was the Creator's dilemma. Should God ignore these creatures? Permit them to continue misbehaving? Punish? Destroy? Allow them to go extinct? The storytellers portray the Creator as considering such courses of action. "The LORD said, 'I will blot out from the earth the human beings that I have made'" (Genesis 6:7a). In fact, Yahweh was so remorseful that God even considers genocide, not only toward the species *Homo sapiens* but also toward other animals, reptiles, insects, and birds. "I will blot out from the earth the human beings I have created—people together with animals and creeping things and birds of the air" (Genesis 6:7b). What was God to do?[31]

---

31. I realize that I am now speaking of these parables as if they describe history. They are parables, certainly, but while the details are tools to help the parable tellers make their point, I do think they believed that their overall point actually occurred in history. That is, they believed, as I do, that they were witnessing a historical shift in human thinking and behavior. They also believed, as I do, that the Creator was stricken with sadness about this shift.

PART III

God's Secondary Mission:
To Heal a Wayward Species

*"Healing is impossible in loneliness;
it is the opposite of loneliness.
Conviviality is healing.
To be healed we must come with all other creatures
to the feast of creation."*

—WENDELL BERRY

Chapter 5
God's Decision: Gospel

Although in the face of humanity's rebellion God apparently considered removing the species *Homo sapiens* from the face of the Earth, God must have eventually decided otherwise—thankfully for us. Perhaps the Deity thought, "Can a mother destroy one of her offspring? Can a father kill one of his children? And why would I act in the manner of Cain?" So instead of eradicating the species *Homo sapiens* (for the sake of the world), God put in motion another plan: God decided to try to heal our species. The Creator determined to mend us and bring us back into restored relationship with and within the community of life. The biblical narrative from Genesis 6:7 onward, both Old and New Testaments, then, is this story. It is the story of a new secondary mission that God decides to undertake. It is a story of profound engagement, mercy, and love. From God's great reservoir of love—*agape, philos,* and *eros*—God resolves to try to doctor human beings back to health by nursing us back into relationship.[32]

God's primary mission—the evolving story of life—had been going on for 13.7 billion years and had always been more than a full-time undertaking. However, in addition to this long-time primary mission, in a profound act of grace, the Creator decided (recently) to also take on a secondary mission. This secondary mission would focus on one species. This mission would be an earnest act of mercy to try to reinstate a lost and wayward species back into the Father's household, so that its members could once again take up responsible residence in the particular dwelling places allotted to them.

The species calls itself *Homo sapiens.* The name for God's decision regarding their restoration is "gospel," or "good news." Not only is God's decision good news for us humans, but it is also good news for the rest of the community of life, which has suffered so much since the beginning of Cain's recent mutiny. This community of life continues to suffer in the twenty-first century, as Cain's voracious appetites over-consume biomass, reduce (oversimplify) diversity, deplete freshwater supplies, poison the atmosphere, deteriorate precious soil, foul the oceans, and extinguish other species at alarming rates.[33] How

---

32. These three Greek words for love point to the scope, quality, and depth of God's love for the world, including humans. *Agape* looks past all that is unlovable in the other. *Philos* is like a deep and abiding friendship. *Eros* is being in love with all that is loveable about the other. In marriage this kind of love enjoys sexual intimacy.

33. Today, scientists estimate that the biomass consumed or spoiled by the world's 7 billion humans causes the extinction of over thirty thousand species annually. This calculation is part of the permanent "Evolving Planet" exhibition at the Field Museum of Natural History in Chicago, as well as other references. It is normal for ten to twenty species per year to naturally become extinct. But currently a staggering eighty species a day are being destroyed forever by us.

would the Creator accomplish this secondary mission?[34] According to these and other inspired storytellers, including those who continue to contribute to the biblical narrative, God's endeavors would take several interesting twists and turns.

---

34. The notion of the Creator simultaneously engaged in two missions, an ancient primary mission that seeks the well-being of the whole world, and a recent secondary mission that is dedicated to healing humans, is an unconventional interpretation within historic Christianity. For me, this approach captures what I take to be powerful intuitions about God's love for the cosmos, for the Earth, for the whole community of life, and for our species.

Chapter 6
Early Attempts

Firstly, God tried a great *flood*. The parable of Noah and the Flood is conveyed in Genesis 6–9. I choose the word "parable" intentionally. In my view, this narrative is not historical. I have several reasons for taking this position. First, no credible department of geology or geosciences in any university or college in the world can find evidence of an Earth-covering flood that took place during the period of human presence on the Earth. Of course, various locales have experienced floods, even devastating ones. Such floods occur seasonally even today, and are necessary elements of God's *tov* garden, nourishing the soil and replenishing precious water tables and aquifers. Some floods have obviously been quite severe and even destructive to creatures residing in these regions, including humans. However, none have been so massive and all-encompassing that the waters "swelled so mightily on the earth that all the high mountains under the whole heaven were covered . . . covering them fifteen cubits deep" (Genesis 7:19–20). The waters certainly never rose higher than 16,802-foot Mount Ararat in Turkey (Genesis 8:4), let alone higher than 29,029 foot Mount Everest in Nepal/Tibet.

Another reason to consider this narrative a parable is that deeming it historical renders the Creator a god of genocide, infanticide, and annihilation. Such a portrayal seems more in line with the character of a Nazi death camp than with major themes in the biblical witness.[35] I personally do not believe or trust in a divine Creator who at one point would massacre all creatures except aquatic life, all the moms and dads, grandmas and grandpas, and boys and girls of the species *Homo sapiens* except one small clan belonging to Noah and his wife, and all land creatures except one male and one female of each species (apparently fish were safe)—even if afterwards God promised never to do it again![36]

There are two significant things to remember about the parable genre in the Bible. The first is that the test of a parable's truthfulness is not whether it actually happened. Parables don't happen in any historical sense. Nathan's parable told to King David about a poor family with a prized lamb (2 Samuel 12:1–7), and Jesus' parables of the sower and the seed (Mark 4:2–20), the Good Samaritan (Luke 10:29–37), the Prodigal Son (Luke 15:11–32), the widow and the unjust judge (Luke 18:1–8), and

---

35. I visited Buchenwald concentration camp at Weimar, Germany in 2010.

36. The narrative in Genesis 6:19–20 and Genesis 7:8–9 reports *one* pair of each animal brought into the Ark. In contrast, Genesis 7:1–5 reports *seven* pairs of clean animals and one pair of unclean animals, and seven pairs of each bird. Every kind of food is to be taken in also, which may refer to vegetation and even insects. As an explanation for the inconsistencies, Biblical scholars understand that these two sections were written by several different writers from different historical periods and were blended later by a scribe, or school of scribes.

the wedding banquet (Matthew 22:1-14), do not relay events that actually occurred. They were not events of the day that a media outlet could have filmed and reported on the evening newscast, or that someone could have posted on YouTube. Yet they are true; utterly so. They open our eyes to see God in profound and new ways. They move our souls to understand ourselves and life itself better. This is an important nuance to grasp if one wants to move beyond Sunday school and towards a more considered engagement with the Bible.

The second thing to remember about parables is that they usually have a point. So what is the point of the Noah and the Flood parable? I suggest the message is this: if we think we can get rid of bad people by killing off bad people, we need to think again. It turns out that Noah and his household picked up the slack of badness almost immediately. In a disturbing episode shortly after they disembarked from the ark, Noah makes a batch of wine, consumes it, becomes fall-down drunk, and drops off to sleep naked in his tent. His second son, Ham, who is the father of Canaan (Genesis 5:32), happens to see his father, Noah, not only smashed, but nude. When he awakens, Noah is so self-loathing at his bad behavior and the fact that it was witnessed "from his wine and [knows] what his son [has] done to him," that he invokes an evil blight upon his son Ham's offspring. "Cursed be Canaan; lowest of slaves shall he be to his brothers" (Genesis 9:24-27). This curse sets in motion nefarious circumstances that for generations consign the descendents of Ham to the status of enslaved chattel. So much for Noah being "a righteous man, blameless in his generation," who "walked with God" (Genesis 6:9).[37]

---

37. We know that many American and European slaveholders referenced this biblical story as a basis for rationalizing their systemic enslavement of African men, women, and children. They fantasized that Africans were the accursed descendents of Ham whom the Bible itself destined for slavery, and then took the next "logical" step.

Next, as the narrative unfolds, God tried making a *chosen people*.[38] (In what follows, I summarize this in a sweeping interpretation of several books in the Old Testament, to be sure.) The idea is that God selected a small number of people to whom God would give opportunities to learn how to live responsibly and faithfully, who would then become a beacon of instruction to others. The prophet Isaiah described the following:

> In the days to come the mountain of the LORD'S house shall be established as the highest of mountains, and shall be raised above the hills; all nations shall stream to it. Many peoples shall say: "Come, let us go up to the mountain of the LORD, to the house of the God of Jacob; that he may teach us his ways and that we may walk in his paths." For out of Zion shall go forth instruction, and the word of the LORD from Jerusalem. He shall judge between the nations and shall arbitrate for many peoples. They shall beat their swords into plowshares and their spears into pruning hooks. Nation shall not lift up sword against nation; neither shall they learn war any more. *Isaiah 2:2–4 (also Micah 4:1–4)*

So God began fashioning a chosen people. Where did God find these people? In the book of Exodus, we read that there was an immigrant tribe of Israelites in Egypt who "groaned under their slavery," and that God "heard the groaning." The Lord "remembered his covenant with Abraham, Isaac, and Jacob . . . took notice of them" (Exodus 2:24), and began

---

38.   Some people may find the idea of God "trying" various strategies to be a demeaning concept. Since God is not working with human objects, but rather human subjects who have "will" (though not "free will" in my view), it makes sense to me to see how God would not be imposing healing and restoration upon any creature as though we were robots. Hence, God must go through a process of trial and error before finding the right remedy.

to put in motion a plan to prepare a leader named Moses to lead this tribe of Israelites to freedom. Arranging their escape from Pharaoh's regime, Yahweh miraculously assisted their crossing of the Sea of Reeds (in Hebrew: *yam suph*), provided water, bread (manna), and meat (quail) to meet their needs, and enrolled them in forty years of "wilderness school" in the Sinai desert. The goal was for these now unfettered people to learn, put into practice, model, and share God's intended way for humans to live honorably in God's garden of life, to live as Abel rather than Cain.[39]

The society in which the Israelites had been living freely at first and later as slaves for 400 years, Pharaoh's Egypt, is a clear example of Cain's worldview and lifestyle. The figure below (see figure 2) is my adaptation of a graphic created by Daniel Erlander of what the system of Takerism looks like.[40]

---

39. The phrase "wilderness school" comes from Daniel Erlanger's wonderful book, *Manna and Mercy*, 7–15.

40. Ibid, 4, 22, 23.

Figure 2: Pharaoh's Egypt • Cain's world

Exodus 1–6

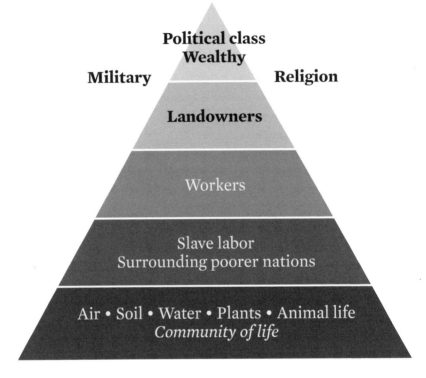

In figure 2, the few who command the system—the political class and landowners, those with means, security, and access—occupy the elitist upper levels. Beneath these top echelons, in increasing population percentages, are the workers such as tradesmen, farmers, teachers, and merchants; then the slaves (and those trapped in jobs paying slave wages). Further down are the surrounding poor nations that Pharaoh entices, bribes, or bullies—whatever it takes—to make sure the natural and human resources of these nations are available to those with money. Pharaoh's upper classes reap most of the wealth from these poorer nations, with meager crumbs, or even less, trickling down to the local inhabitants. Finally, at the bottom level, are the ecosystems and the wider community of life bearing the brunt of Cain/Pharaoh's engulfing structures and systems.

Figure 2 also reminds us that the twin keepers and sanctifiers of Pharaoh/Cain/Takerism's pyramid usually are military power and religion. *Military power*—in today's system, the armies, navies, air forces, marines, civilian support systems, weapons manufacturers, lobbyists—serves as the leveraging apparatus for overtly and covertly bending the world in Cain's favor. This is accomplished through force, the threat of force, and the appearance of the threat of force by means of a robust weapons industry. Military power is essential in achieving and securing the pyramid system.

Religion is the other arm serving in tandem with military power. Religion provides cover and sanctification for the systems of Pharaoh/Cain/Takerism. It allows Cain to see his way of life as ordained by God. Any change to the divine order must be resisted, by force if necessary; for to oppose Pharaoh's Egypt is to oppose God. In Pharaoh's Egypt and Cain's world, these two arms, religion and the military, serve as the witting and unwitting tools of the powers and principalities.[41]

As the biblical narrative continues, Yahweh sets the enslaved Hebrews in Egypt free. It is important to remember that Yahweh did not set Israel free in order that Israel might be free. Indeed, freedom can be a false god, just like anything else. Individuals, groups, and nations have committed terrible atrocities and even despoiled their own values in the name of acquiring or protecting freedom. Likewise, Yahweh didn't liberate the people in order that they might "move up the ladder," so to speak. It might have been tempting for them to wish that "next time, *we* will be the ones on top and others will be beneath us." But this was not Yahweh's intent. Rather, Yahweh set the people free so that they would learn and model

---

41. We will explore the phrase "powers and principalities" in chapter 9.

a substitute way of being in God's world. God set Israel free to be an alternative community, an alternative to the pyramid scheme in figure 2.

We can see the entire Old Testament, then, as a saga describing Israel's struggle between God's life-enriching ways of *tov* and Pharaoh's homicidal/suicidal paths of perishing. At times, Israel is faithful to God, and the human community and the Earth rejoices. At other times it falls back under the perilous spell of Pharaoh's dominator and domineering habits.

During the years following Israel's exodus from Egypt, the emancipated people of Israel played out this saga as they endeavored to live the Lord's alternative way. There was a delegation rather than concentration of power.[42] The people sought to love the Lord their God with all their hearts, souls, minds, and strength, and their neighbors as themselves.[43] They lifted up regard for strangers and foreigners, for Israel, too, had been a stranger and foreigner in Egypt. People acknowledged the expectation to care for widows, orphans, and the poor as the ordinary and normal thing to do. Prophets and others were able to constructively criticize leaders, a sign of health in any society. The Jubilee Code was established, which not only elevated the Sabbath day as a day of rest for all creatures, including humans, but also made every seventh year, called the Sabbath year, a year of "solemn rest for the land" (Leviticus

---

42. Moses's father-in-law, Jethro, appears to have been responsible for much of this Abel-like organizational structure that was based on a vigorous sharing of power. See Exodus 18:13–27.

43. This summary of the first three commandments is known as the "shema" in Deuteronomy 6:4–5. Jesus also addressed how the next seven commandments speak of proper relations with our neighbors (Mark 12:28–31).

25:4).[44] And the seventh Sabbath year, the fiftieth year, became the celebrated year of Jubilee. In the Jubilee year, people were restored to their former lands as a reminder that ownership belongs to God rather than property owners (Leviticus 25:10–17).

For about 250 years the community of Israel understood themselves to be a contrast society to the exploitative systems of Egypt and tried to model the partnership values of Abel. Certainly, we should not romanticize this time; this culture was neither perfection nor paradise. There was a back and forth struggle. The pattern recorded in the book of Judges shows several cycles of idolatry, divine punishment, an appeal for help, the emergence of a leader, all followed by periods of Abel living. But even though Israel often fell back into Pharaoh's ways, it was generally a time when Israel understood that its mission was to live differently, to carve out an alternative way of being in God's world. They understood that God's intention for humanity was that they live in relationship with their neighbor, especially the stranger, outcast, and alien, with the Creation, with their own inner spirit/souls/selves, and with the ground of all that was, is, and is to come, the Creator.

Toward the end of this period, during the time of Samuel, a monumental change began to occur. In 1 Samuel 8:1–22, the elders of Israel came to the prophet Samuel with the request that he appoint a king to govern them "like other nations." This was a new concept for Israel. Apparently some of the Israel-

---

44. Scott Gustafson writes, "It is not clear if everyone observes the Sabbath year at the same time. The Sabbath year could have been a system of crop rotation whereby a farmer would not plant one seventh of his land each year. It is clear, however, that the Sabbath year had humanitarian as well as ecological purposes. During the Sabbath year, the owner of the land allows foreigners, slaves, hired men, and domestic and wild animals to harvest what grew in uncultivated fields (Leviticus 25:6–7). The Sabbath year partially restores the sort of culture in existence before the agricultural revolution. In this year, food grows wild. Food is not a commodity. Food is not bought and sold. Food is not placed under 'lock and key.'" Scott W. Gustafson, *Biblical Amnesia*, 53.

ites had been watching their neighbors and noticed that, on the surface, they seemed to have a finer life—with more power, more prestige, and more material appliances. Maybe it was because they have a king, they reasoned. Samuel tried to talk them out of it, but they persisted. In a prayer to Yahweh, Samuel fretted that the Israelites were rejecting his authority. As the biblical text conveys, Yahweh, however, said, "They have not rejected you, but they have rejected *me* from being king over them" (1 Samuel 8:7, emphasis added). This was a major instance of the people making the choice of "forsaking me and serving other gods" (1 Samuel 8:8).

The Lord, through Samuel, warned the people of the dangers and hazards of monarchy. In the following passage, he describes the under-belly of the monarchial/Pharaoh/Cain/Taker system:

> "These will be the ways of the king who will reign over you: he will take your sons and appoint them to his chariots and to be his horsemen, and to run before his chariots; and he will appoint for himself commanders of thousands and commanders of fifties, and some to plow his ground and to reap his harvest, and to make his implements of war and the equipment of his chariots. He will take your daughters to be perfumers and cooks and bakers. He will take the best of your fields and vineyards and olive orchards and give them to his courtiers. He will take one-tenth of your grain and of your vineyards and give it to his officers and courtiers. He will take your male and female slaves, and the best of your cattle and donkeys, and put them to his work. He will take one-tenth of your flocks and you shall be his slaves. And in that day you will cry out because of your king, whom you have chosen for yourselves; but he will not answer you in that day" (1 Samuel 8:11–18).

Despite these warnings, the Israelites proceeded, and in

due course a monarchy was established to rule over the land and over the culture of Israel.

Israel's first king, Saul, known for his prowess as a military leader, was in office from approximately 1,020 BCE to 1,000 BCE (1 Samuel 13–31). His reign began reasonably well, but soon grew foul, as he became obsessed with jealously and suspicion and was tormented by "an evil spirit from the Lord" (1 Samuel 16:14). Wounded in a battle against the Philistine people on Mount Gilboa, he committed suicide by falling on his own sword. Some strains of the biblical tradition portray Saul's life as coming to a noble but tragic end. Other biblical writers, probably wanting to glorify his successor, David, portray Saul as utterly unworthy, deserving of his unhappy fate.

David was the next king, ruling from 1,000 BCE to 961 BCE (2 Samuel 9–20; 1 Kings 1–2). Again, this monarchy began with high hopes and expectations for wonderful things to come, but soon dissolved into spiritual and material corruption. The disturbing episode of David's rape of a married woman named Bathsheba and the subsequent murder of her husband, Uriah the Hittite, was not only a story of personal moral failure, it was also a metaphor of how, beneath Cain's prosperous and even religious veneer, there lurked a system of exploitation, deceit, and death.[45]

David's son, Solomon, followed David's kingship. Solomon reigned as king of Israel from 961 BCE to 922 BCE (1 Kings

---

45. The word "rape" might seem controversial but likely is appropriate. Surely a woman summoned by an all powerful king for immediate sex is not on equal and consensual footing. After seeing her taking a bath naked, and even finding out that she was married, "David sent messengers to get her, and she came to him, and he lay with her" (2 Samuel 11:4). The word "murder" also seems fitting. When King David's behavior produced a pregnancy in Bathsheba, David tried several schemes to cover it up, including orchestrating a war battle and seeing that Bathsheba's husband is placed at the front. "In the morning David wrote a letter to Joab, and sent it by the hand of Uriah. In the letter he wrote, 'Set Uriah in the forefront of the hardest fighting, and then draw back from him so that he may be struck down and die'" (2 Samuel 11:14–15).

1–11). His administration also began with high hopes. In fact, his precocious prayer as a young boy at the beginning of his sovereignty is even quite touching: "O Lord my God, you have made your servant king in place of my father David, although I am only a little child; I do not know how to go out or come in. And your servant is in the midst of the people whom you have chosen, a great people, so numerous they cannot be numbered or counted. Grant your servant therefore an understanding mind to govern your people, able to discern between good and evil; for who can govern this your great people"? The Lord was pleased that Solomon took up his weighty responsibility with this tone of humility (1 Kings 3:7–10). But soon Solomon became corrupted as well. Not only did he become a conquistador of material wealth, the terror of Israel's neighbors with his armies, and a self-centered concupiscent with 700 wives and 300 girlfriends (concubines)[46], he also ordered the construction of a glorious religious temple, supposedly in honor of Yahweh, using subjugated slaves. "King Solomon conscripted forced labor out of all Israel; the levy numbered thirty thousand men" (1 Kings 5: 13). It is hard to imagine a greater contradiction of God's values.

In an ironic and tragic twist of history, the people's experiment with monarchy thoroughly impeded the nascent development of Israel's character and faith. The leaders of Israel soon became dominators, bullying and exploiting the land's occupants as well as surrounding peoples. The rich had too much for their own good; the poor, too little. The blood of Abel cried out from the ground (Genesis 4:10) under the weight of oppression. In less than one hundred years, everything had come full circle. Israel's king had become just another Pharaoh, and Israel itself just another Egypt. (Again, see

---

46. "King Solomon loved many foreign women along with the daughter of Pharaoh . . . Among Solomon's wives were seven hundred princesses and three hundred concubines" (1 Kings 11:1, 3).

figure 2 on page 58.)

In concert with this experiment of creating a chosen people, God also instituted *laws*, the imparting and implementation of which were part of God's agenda for the Israelites during their schooling in the Sinai wilderness. There was the Priestly Code emphasizing religious and ritual concerns, and the covenant code dealing with civil law. There was a Holiness Code (Leviticus 17–26) describing purity and holy living, and the laws in Deuteronomy which dealt with everything from the Ten Commandments to remarriage to waging holy war. Laws are important, as we know, and cultures need them; as the apostle Paul stated, law "is holy and just and good" (Romans 7:12). But these instruments also fell short in healing the species. Laws often brought out the worst in people. Some people became legalistic, others self-righteous, and still others followed the letter of the law but missed its depth and spirit. Furthermore, knowing that a rule prohibits certain behaviors sometimes impelled people to actually want to do those behaviors.[47] So it was with many Israelites.

We also know from history that law can become a formidable tool of Cain's violence. Historically, and in our own time, the law has been used to oppress women, deny basic rights to gay and lesbian couples and individuals, steal land and decimate cultures of indigenous peoples, and brutalize enemies.

---

47.   This might be the primary lesson of the prohibition experiment in the United States. From the time the 18th Amendment (Volstead Act) prohibiting alcohol took effect on January 17, 1920, to its rescinding through passage of the 22nd Amendment (Cullen-Harrison Act) on December 5, 1933, a colossal network of organized crime sprang up around the country turning ordinary people into callous criminals. In New York City alone there were fifty thousand illegal speakeasies, and even elected officials and policemen were breaking the law.

During the long centuries of white enslavement of Africans in the United States of America, people justified lynching a man who "stole" a loaf of bread by reference to the law, with little admission that they who did the lynching actually stole the person's life. Judges, policemen, government officials, and school boards carried out terrible deeds under the law, with most deeming their decision to enforce these statutes as justifiable and even honorable.

The powerful have used laws to authorize the pollution of water and air, the injection of harmful chemicals into agriculture, the treatment of animals with disregard, and the destruction of pristine forests, wetlands, and soils. The law has been used to fabricate spurious justifications for warfare, including preemptive war. Law even carried out the crucifixion of the Christ of God.

Some laws, such as those of the Sabbath and Jubilee Codes, were profound examples of Abel living. They showed deep respect for neighbor, creation, and God. But as in our own culture today, the people of Israel found ways around these blessings and likely never really implemented them on a large scale.

Yahweh's final major attempt to heal Cain's sickness involved dispatching *prophets*. These messengers had the eyes and ears to perceive what was really happening beneath Takerism's veneer. They had the courage to speak up about what they saw, and were able to alarm and frighten the people into shaping up. But this approach harbored a problem: while prophetic warnings worked initially, the threat level was impossible as well as imprudent to sustain indefinitely. Once the crisis diminished, people quickly returned to their former Cain/Taker thinking and behavior. Furthermore, Cain/Taker tendencies became worse after a season of heightened I-centeredness due to the anxiety caused by trying to save one's own skin.

These early experiments—involving a flood (parable), chosen people, law, kings, and prophets—while important and containing some value, ultimately fell short in God's secondary mission. Humanity was still on the loose, still living out of relationship, and still causing harm. What was the Creator to do? Is there any way to repair and restore this species? We will next look at a bold new action on God's part, one that became incarnate in the life, ministry, death, and resurrection of Jesus of Nazareth.

Chapter 7
The Embodied Message of
Abel of Nazareth

During the centuries following the Fall, which began as far back as 9,000 to 5,000 years ago, and began to be addressed in the Genesis narratives about 3,000 years ago, God introduced many Abels into the human population. Sometimes Abel came in the form of a rabbi, prophet, wise woman or wise man, or even in the form of people sequestered to the margins by society, such as outcasts and sinners. At other times, Abel came as a member of the wider community of life—animals, vegetation, waters, and winds—and other "still small voices" beckoning for us to return. The missions of these Abels were the same: to try to restore Cain to the Creator's household with and within the community of life under the permeating reign of God.

But as Cain's advance of clutter and noise escalated, more and more cultures became inept at seeing what was occurring and of comprehending what it all meant. "Eyes to see and ears to hear" no longer worked as before, as both ethical and spiritual capacities diminished among all who succumbed. The Creator's dilemma grew more dire.

Finally, according to the biblical narrative, God decided to come in person. This was a monumental shift in the Deity's modus operandi. God had never done this before. However, the Creator could not actually show up in person. Why? Because God's stature was too big; God's presence was too awesome; God's light was too bright. Had the Deity appeared as fully God, every organism with cellular membranes would have imploded, struck by staggering fear, and every creature with a heart would have exploded into an artery-bursting *acute myocardial infarction* (heart attack). The Deity's presence in person would have been too thoroughly overwhelming and comprehensively overpowering.

So instead of coming in person, the Deity emptied self of self and very God of very God, and became human. In his letter to the Philippians, the apostle Paul put his version of this incarnation (enfleshment) into liturgical form by describing Jesus the Christ as one who, "though he was in the form of God, did not regard equality with God as something to be grasped, but *emptied* himself, taking the form of a slave, being born in human likeness" (2:6–7, emphasis added).

But why did God elect to become a human creature? Obviously the Lord is not a member of any created species, including *Homo sapiens*. Why would God choose to become one of us? Conceivably, if horses had been the malfunctioning species, a horse would have been born in Bethlehem. Or if ants, or bacteria, or red-winged blackbirds, or even dolphins had been as rebellious as humans, we would be telling a very different story. But all these species were (are) doing fine. They were living reasonably well in the dwelling places allotted them with and within the community of life in the Creator's household under the permeating reign of God. So why did God decide to become human? Why choose our species? Because it was the human creature that was lost, and the Christ of God came "to seek and to save the lost."

Abel of Nazareth was born in Bethlehem twenty centuries ago. This is recent history compared to the history of our species (a history that spans two thousand centuries) and even more so when compared to the vast and ancient story of life. (Again, see figure 1 on page 12.) As this son of God imparted God's gospel, he moved about the region of Galilee, Samaria, and Judea, a tiny parcel of land on the eastern edge of the Mediterranean Sea. As he went out, he proclaimed a message of monumental simplicity and transforming power. The message was (is) this: "*Homo sapiens,* you are forgiven; repent, and follow me." This message-made-flesh in Abel of Nazareth is the gospel, or good news (in Greek: *eu-angellion*), of Jesus Christ. This embodied message is the content and spiritual electricity of God's story of Jesus. It is simple, profound, and loaded with consequence.

Firstly, this proclamation embodied boundless forgiveness. "*Homo sapiens*, you are forgiven." With these words, Jesus, in effect, said, "Humans, you are forgiven for your I-centered-ness. You are exonerated for living as though you are separate from, superior to, the reason for, and the rulers of the rest of my community of life. You are absolved from condemnation for supplanting the Creator's household under the reign of God with your own house and your own reign. You are released from the guilt of de-evolving as a species, and from the waste of aimlessly wandering the Earth in a stupor of out of relationship destruction." In short, God decided to meet humanity's mutiny with grace.

However, forgiveness was not God's ultimate goal, and forgiveness alone is not the gospel of Jesus Christ. God wasn't saying, "I forgive you *Homo sapiens*; now everything is fine. Sure, you are at war with your neighbors, my creation, your inner spirit, and with me, but you are forgiven. Now, go write a cacophony of praise songs and liturgies telling me how wonderful you think I am to forgive you for messing up my world." No, this act of absolution by itself was not God's gospel and justice in Christ. Rather, God's ultimate goal was the transformation of our species.

One might wish that forgiveness would have been enough. It would have been nice if this simple declaration had brought instant—or even eventual—healing, reconciliation, and restoration. And we may wonder, why not? Surely we know that an all-powerful God can say, "Let it be," and it will be so. Surely God's reign can have its way with any creature, including humans. However, we also know that durable healing and true restoration doesn't happen with the snap of a finger, a bop on the forehead, or even a forceful declaration. Rather, true healing is a process, a path, a way.

So accompanying the extension of God's abiding gift of forgiveness, Jesus also declared/invited/commanded, "Repent." The word "repent" (in Greek: *metanoia*) means "turn around." To understand this word, it is also helpful to understand another Greek word, *hamartia*, which is one of the words for sin. Sin in this case means "off the mark." Imagine a target on a wall with a center bull's-eye surrounded by concentric circles. Hitting the center, or mark, is good. Hitting farther away from the center makes one more and more "off the mark." A person or species in need of repentance is one who is so wrong headed, and so lost in the direction they are going, that they can't even *see* the target. The target is east, and they are facing west. It is forward, and they are turned backward. So Jesus commands us to repent, that is, to turn around completely from the direction of Cain/Takerism. This is not a mere fine-tuning or tweaking, but a complete one hundred eighty degree about-face. "Repent, for the kingdom (reign) of God is at hand" (Matthew 3:2; 4:17; 10:7).

In order to finish this metabolically embodied message of forgiveness and the call to turn around (repent), Jesus also had one more thing to declare/invite/command: "Follow me." Not just follow *me*, as opposed to following false gods such as riches, status, technology, or self, but also *follow* me, as opposed to staying where we are. Jesus wants us to go with him. Jesus wants us to leave the place of perishing in which we stand and go to a place of life. Jesus wants us to physically journey somewhere with him, to "go and learn what this means" (Matthew 9:13). But where, Lord, we might ask? Follow you *where*? To this Jesus responds,

- "Follow me to meet your neighbor." For Jesus, my neighbor is not just a person I like or a person like me, but also and especially strangers (strange ones?), outcasts (those discarded), and aliens (illegal aliens?). My neighbor is even my enemy. "Come with me," Jesus says, "to meet and be restored into relationship with your estranged human neighbor."[48]

- Also he says, "Follow me to meet the Creation. *Homo sapiens*, you are not doing very well. You daily show disregard for my Father's beloved world. You overconsume, overpollute, and bring species to extinction at alarming rates. There is a denigration of God's primary mission going on in your ranks. There is a groaning in travail in my creation and I have heard their cries. Turn around, *Homo sapiens*, and follow me. You have much to learn and there is a more excellent way. I will go with you into restored

---

48. See appendix C for a sermon by my daughter on God's mission to help us restore healthy relationship with our neighbors.

and respectful relationship within the ecosystems and with the life-forms of God's cherished and *tov* world."[49]

- Also, "Follow me to meet your own inner spirit/souls/selves." Humans are plagued with not only other-alienation, but also self-alienation. We behave as though we have little respect for our deepest souls, the *tov* beings that the Creator has made and loves just as he loves all other creatures.

- And finally, "Follow me; I want you to meet my Mother/Father. Mutiny and I-centeredness (anthropo-narcissism) is killing you and disengaging you from all that is of God. Come to the source; come to the truth. Learn again what it means to embrace the source of life and to live the prayer, "Hallowed be thy name" (Matthew 6:9).

Christians, then, are people who don't just follow *Jesus*, but who *follow* Jesus. Not his teachings; not vague principles; not even so much what he did back in biblical times. In this sense, Christians are not WWJD (what would Jesus do?) bracelet wearers. Why? Because Jesus is not back in biblical times. Easter means he is alive today in the twenty-first century. He is here and now and bids every human person to follow him into

---

49. "Biomimicry" (from *bios*, meaning life, and *mimesis*, meaning to imitate) is a fascinating design approach that seeks to learn from and emulate nature. It looks at the ways other species and ecosystems have been imaginative by necessity in their time-tested ways of acquiring food, moving about, reproducing, and dealing with waste. It asks, how does nature do it? This approach has found that by and large nature runs on sunlight, uses only the energy it needs, rewards cooperation, recycles everything, thrives on diversity, form fits function, uses local expertise, curbs excess, and is generally handsome. Biomimicry looks at nature, rather than humans, as model, mentor, and measure.

restored relationship this day.[50] Christians are people who do this. Not only do we have the gratitude to receive God's forgiveness, and not only do we have the trust in God to repent (turn around), but we also have the courage, or are willing to pray for the courage, to physically move our feet and travel with a risen Christ today into locations and situations wherein we will encounter neighbors, creation, the inner spirit, and God. Within this movement, this "way, truth, and life" (John 14:6) comes a holy transformation from estrangement to reconciliation, from a "sickness unto death"[51] to healing, from being lost to being found, and from perishing to being saved.

Back in the second chapter, I indicated that death and dying are part of God's creation. All that lives eventually dies. Life and death and death and life are the norm in God's *tov* garden and this is the way God intended it to be. But if death is not an evil thing, and if Jesus didn't come to bring an end to it on planet Earth, why did he come? If not for this, what? The answer is this: Jesus came to overcome not death, but *perishing*. To be caught up in perishing is different than to experience death. To be in a state of perishing is to be out of relationship with one's neighbor, especially the stranger, outcast, alien, and enemy. To be in a state of perishing is to be out of relationship

---

50. Jesus' call to follow him back in biblical times related intimately to the issues of those days. Moving toward relationship with neighbor, creation, inner spirit, and with God meant certain things for Jews and others living under the oppression of Roman-occupied Palestine. Today, Jesus' call will be intimately related to the issues of our day. In Palestine today, for example, it just might be that the Jewish state is now the occupier and oppressor rather than the victim. How is Jesus calling people to move from being out-of-relationship to relationship living today?

51. "Sickness unto death" is a Søren Kierkegaard phrase meaning despair of spirit. See Charles E. Moore, ed. *Provocations: Spiritual Writings of Kierkegaard*, 133–135.

with God's creation—to "trample it with harden soles." To be in a state of perishing is to be out of relationship with one's own inner spirit/soul/self. And to perish is to be out of relationship with the source, ground, and destination of all that is, the Creator. With this image in mind then, conceivably someone could be walking around alive today and still be perishing, while another person might have died this very morning and not be perishing at all. At times the biblical writers, including the apostle Paul, seem to intimate that the reality of death and dying in this world is an enemy. I'm suggesting that they are perhaps referring to not death per se, but perishing.

Chapter 8
What about Heaven and Hell?

The concepts of heaven and hell occupy people's minds to varying degrees. I personally do not spend a lot of time contemplating these ideas, but I have considered them from time to time as I've traveled my journey.

Jesus calls us to follow him into the saving joy of restored relationship with neighbors, creation, inner spirit, and God. Obviously, we will not fulfill this process in our lifetimes. We all have areas of continued brokenness, conflict, relapse, and emptiness. This might be where the concept of heaven comes in. Some Christians think of heaven as a place of eternal bliss, or even of reward; many of the old time gospel hymns carry these themes. I see heaven as a place where the healing process progresses, though with fewer encumbrances than we experience in this life.

In 1999, Anglican bishop and Nobel Peace prize recipient

Desmond Tutu wrote a remarkable book called *No Future Without Forgiveness*. In this book, Tutu describes the work of South Africa's Truth and Reconciliation Commission (TRC). Nelson Mandela established this commission after he was elected president of South Africa in April 1994 in the country's first ever democratic election. I happened to be in Johannesburg, South Africa, the week before this historic vote and was deeply moved by the courage, spirit of forgiveness, and electric hope stirring among the people. The TRC's assignment was to facilitate reconciliation between the various factions in the land. It was to mete out not punishment, not revenge, and not hatred, but reconciliation. Certainly, the African people had legitimate cause for vengeance toward their white invaders and oppressors. The three-hundred-year suffering inflicted upon them by the forces of racism and apartheid was unforgiveable. If ever there were a circumstance for which accountability, punishment, and even revenge might be justified, this was it. However, President Mandela and Bishop Tutu knew a deeper truth, namely that punishment and settling scores don't bring reconciliation. They only add fuel to the fire of further conflagrations.

So the TRC took a bold step and decided to grant full amnesty for every crime committed in the name and spirit of apartheid. The only condition for receiving such forgiveness was *courage*. Each state terrorist and each government official who perpetrated decades of intimidation, harassment, torture, murder, hate, and lynching upon African families, as well as those African citizens who committed violence in the process of trying to fight back to save their land and people, would no longer face indictment, trial, conviction, or punishment. All could receive amnesty, full and clear. They simply had to come into a courtroom and meet face-to-face and soul-with-soul the persons they had harmed.

This process set in motion powerful and emotional events. Government terrorists publically confessed their actions in the presence of the very persons whom they had terrorized, or their surviving loved ones. Enemies heard words spoken from wounded souls and looked into the eyes of traumatized brothers and sisters. Government, police, and military crimes were lifted from behind the veil of secrecy into the light of day. Missing persons who had mysteriously disappeared into apartheid's gulags and graveyards were accounted for. Tears flowed, forgiveness found expression, hearts opened, and reconciliation began. Through the often-painful process of truth telling, many received the blessing of soulful liberation. Again, the only requirement was courage. As the scenario played out over the weeks and months, it became apparent to most that not only was forgiveness necessary for healing to occur, but it was also never a solo event or a one-way street. Rather, it was at least bi-lateral, and often multi-lateral and ongoing. And it didn't work to say, "I forgive you, but I never want to see you again!" No, the process of forgiveness only came to fruition as souls were met and relationships were restored and the parties were able to go forward together.

Of course, this doesn't mean that both sides were equally at fault. In South Africa, as in the history of slavery and racism in our own country, the apartheid forces were exponentially the greater evil. There is never parity between oppressor and oppressed. The two sides do not carry the same ethical weight. However, the oppressed victims of South Africa's apartheid took up an equal burden in the offering of forgiveness, in the restoring of relationship, and in the process of national healing.[52]

---

52. I hesitate to use the word "national" is this context, since it was the European powers in the late 1800s who partitioned the continent of Africa and imposed, in many cases brutally, today's national borders. This was done with no regard for the diversity and uniqueness of various African ethnic groups, cultures, and traditions. Nevertheless, the vast arrays of ethnic groups in South Africa (there are 22 different languages) seem committed to trying to become a nation.

This is how I have come to view heaven. It is a place of inner healing and intra-healing. Heaven is different than this life, to be sure. Coveting won't be allowed. Nor will greed, racism, war departments, self-centeredness, or pollution.[53] And there will be plenty of time to immerse ourselves in what it takes for relationships to be truly restored, namely time and courage. But in heaven, captors will meet captives on equal footing. Bomber pilots, weapons manufacturers, and drone executioners will look into the eyes of the grandmas and grandpas, moms and dads, and boys and girls whose flesh they set ablaze, legs they crushed, bodies they severed, and homes they left in rubble. Polluters (from large corporations to individual households) will embrace the arms of an aching creation. A soldier will hug the mother and father of the daughter or son he killed. Over-consumers will lie down next to the child who is starving and the lake that is choking from pollution. And healing will come.

Again, true healing doesn't happen with the snap of a finger. It is a process, a practice, a way of being. Some of this healing can take place in this life, surely, but heaven will be an unfettered realm. Another way to say it is this: "Now we see in a mirror, dimly: then we will see face to face. Now [we] know in part; then [we] will know fully, even as [we] have been fully known" (1 Corinthians 13:12). And this formidable process will be so compelling and the results so liberating that it might be best described as a heavenly banquet or a feast of victory; a blessing and even a new Jerusalem; a river overflowing with the renewing waters of life; and a tree whose leaves are for the healing of the nations.

---

53.   Rob Bell's book *Love Wins,* is a worthy read on the topic of heaven and hell.

What about hell? Of course, unfortunately, some individuals summoned by the Truth and Reconciliation Commission were unable to find courage within their own souls and were incapable of reaching out for help. Some perhaps even preferred to remain estranged from their neighbors. The benefits of Takerism can be so illusory, especially in the seductive notions of superiority and deniability they afford, that people will sometimes walk away from the "entering into relationship" that forgiveness requires.[54] Those who rejected the TRC's offer of amnesty were not able to comprehend the joy of reconciliation. Absenting themselves from this holy blessing, they chose instead a hellish existence, the effects of which will likely and sadly be passed onto their offspring. Perhaps this is the meaning of the biblical prognosis that it is the children who suffer most, often unto the third and fourth generations, from the iniquities of parents who reject God's ways and wisdom (Deuteronomy 5:9).

Sadly, there will probably be some members of *Homo sapiens* who will not have the courage, or the capacity to ask for God's, their neighbor's, or creation's help in finding the courage, to meet those they harmed or who harmed them in this life. Nor will they wish to. Some will refuse this terrible and sweet gift. Some will repudiate the miracle of a restored relationship with their neighbor, especially their enemy. Some will want to retain their imagined superiority and continue their part in humanity's warfare against creation. In so doing, the holy process of healing will be truncated, leaving only hell. This abyss of isolation won't be meted out by the Creator, but

---

54. When Jesus invited a wealthy man to consider a more ethical way of living, the man said no thanks and walked away, "for he had many possessions" (Luke 18:18–23).

rather will be self-imparted.[55]

---

55. After a class I taught, a woman shared her story. She, along with several
     other women, had been attacked and raped by a man who was subsequently
     apprehended. After several years in prison, the man was up for parole. The
     judge invited the women to meet their attacker and tell him their stories
     of grief. The prisoner refused to meet with them; it was too painful, and he
     couldn't find the courage. For the time being, he chose to remain in hell.
         I also spoke with a man whose ancestors had been slave-holders in a
     Southern state, who had even murdered the men, women, and children
     they held in bondage at the end of the Civil War rather than give up their
     enslavement entitlements. He and his relatives *today* still believe "states'
     rights" were violated in the ending of slavery, the ending of Jim Crow, the
     ending of segregation, the Voting Rights Act of 1964, and continued national
     impositions of justice against the will of the majority in a particular state.
     Most of them referred to themselves as Christians. Cain's worldview dies
     neither quickly nor easily.

PART IV

Opponents to God's Mission

*"It's surprising how much memory
is built around things unnoticed at the time."*

—Barbara Kingsolver

Chapter 9
Powers and Principalities

This book is one person's attempt to rethink, reframe, and recast the narrative of God's story of life and God's story of Jesus. My thesis is that historic Christianity needs reconsideration. It is small, it is I-centered, and it is unduly enamored with the species *Homo sapiens*. Christianity itself needs to find God's larger truth again. On this ongoing personal expedition of faith, I have attempted to do this by re-envisioning God's ancient and vast story of life in light of both the sciences of the past 450 years and Earth's (including humanity's) ancient wisdom, and by placing the narrative of Jesus within this larger context.

I've also argued that God's recently initiated secondary mission to heal a wayward species is directed at humans. It is for us and about us only. However, it is not for and about us

because we are so special or exalted. We are not the most important species on planet Earth, and we are not the most important
species in God's heart. Rather, God's secondary mission is for
and about us because we are a species that has grown inimical
to God's primary mission (the story of life) and we are in grave
need of transformation.[56]

Ironically, Christianity has become part of the problem.
In the course of the church's meanderings through the past
twenty centuries of history, the actions of Christians in many
cultures have become almost indistinguishable from the ways
of Cain/Takerism. Not only do we not reflect the wholeness of
God's primary mission and God's love for the cosmos well, but
we also have twisted the intent of God's secondary mission. In
fact, we have become so confused in our I-centeredness that
many Christians, historically and today, regard the needs and
desires of *Homo sapiens sapiens* as God's *primary* concern. In
so doing, Christians have made Christianity into just another
form of "humanism."

By humanism, I mean that Christianity has shrunk. It has
withered into a diminutive melodrama about how much God
gushes over *us*. "God loves you soooo . . . much," the preacher
oozes (I've preached this many times, too). In fact, the more *o*'s
in the word "so," the larger the congregation or denomination
seems destined to multiply in membership. If a congregation is
also clever enough to add to the human exceptionalist ideology

---

56. I realize that I disagree with the viewpoints of certain biblical writers,
including the one who wrote Psalm 8. This person, who rightly is awestruck
that God would take the time to care a hoot about humans, concludes
therefore that God must have made humans "a little lower than God, and
crowned them with glory and honor" (verses 4–5). This writer also believes
God has given humans "dominion over the works of your hands; you have put
all things under their feet, all sheep and oxen, and also the beasts of the field,
the birds of the air, and the fish of the sea, whatever passes along the paths
of the seas" (verses 6–9). Again, I disagree with this viewpoint, and believe
instead that God cherishes humans as God cherishes all of creation, and that
the notions of human exceptionalism and dominion are detrimental. This
will be further explored in the next paragraphs.

("it's all about us") an unapologetic dosage of national exceptionalism ("the United States is the greatest nation on the face
of the Earth . . . the best country the world has ever known"),
and an unequivocal declaration of Christian exceptionalism
("our religion is better than yours")[57], the troika for success in
Cain's culture is complete. However, in my view, while such a
church will likely be grand, wealthy, and influential, it will also
be something other than a church of God. It will be something
other than a forgiven community of *Homo sapiens* turning
around (repenting) and following the risen Christ into restored
relationship with neighbor, creation, inner spirit/soul/self, and
the Creator. It will be something other than a restored community brought back into the Father's house to take up residence
in the dwelling places allotted the human creature with and
within the wider community of life under the permeating
reign of God. It will be just another form of humanism, that is,
a human-focused worldview.[58]

The problem is that there are forces at work in the world
that do not want our species to be healed, that do not want us
to be successfully transformed from perishing to fullness of life.
The apostle Paul, in the sixth chapter of Ephesians, describes

---

57. In *A New Kind of Christianity: Ten Questions That Are Transforming the
     Faith*, Brian McLaren pens a chapter entitled "How Should Followers of
     Jesus Relate to People of Other Religions?" McLaren rightly reminds us that
     "Christianity has a nauseating, infuriating, depressing record when it comes
     to encountering people of other religions" (p. 208). "Like a gunslinger going
     for his revolver," Christians often "reach for John 14:6 and draw it in a flash,"
     boasting triumphantly, "didn't Jesus say he was the way, truth, and life and
     the only way to the Father?" End of discussion. McLaren's chapter 19 is a
     worthy read. Not only does he do a superb job of disarming the gunslinger
     mentality, he also presents both a much humbler assessment of Christianity
     and a larger understanding of the worldview of Jesus.

58. Ironically, it is the more conservative/fundamentalist churches that are the
     most extreme manifestations of "humanism."

such forces as "powers and principalities."[59] Sometimes these powers take the form of persons or groups. Other times they are systemic, ideological, and cultural. They are spiritual, certainly, and they are often subliminal. However, their tenacious commitment is to create and maintain a world where relationship *impairment* flourishes.

There are reasons for this. Remaining out of relationship with one's *neighbor* strengthens power-based dichotomies, such as insiders versus outsiders, haves versus have-nots, those considered worthy and those rendered less so, and us versus them. Remaining out of relationship with the stranger, outcast, and alien also works to feed the flourishing war industry. This industry relies on war's perpetual motion and emotion, including continuous weapons research and development and an attending arms dealing around the globe (sometimes to both sides in a conflict). These powers and principalities consider war-making not just a horrifying sin of last resort, something of which we can never be proud, but an acceptable, and if done right, responsible and even glorious tool of governance. They know that warfare and its endless prospects foster (short-term) job growth. They know that the patriotism it engenders consolidates political power. And they know that at war's end, there will be an almost endless supply of government contracts needing to be dispersed, mostly to the friends of whomsoever is in power at the time, to clean up the devastation and restock the arsenal. Restocking the arsenal is especially titillating, since there are always new technologies to bring out. These tech-

---

59. "For our struggle is not against the enemies of blood and flesh, but against the rulers, against the authorities, against the cosmic powers of this present darkness, against the principalities of evil in the heavenly places" (Ephesians 6:12).

nologies excite and arouse Takerism's enthusiastic members.[60]

Glorification of war also saturates the Hollywood entertainment and computer-gaming industries, ensuring Takerism's spiritual grip on the next generation. The big and small screens work diligently to affix to Cain's affections for warfare such laudable concepts as valor, heroism, loyalty, honor, adventure, faith, commitment, and being the best man or woman one can be.[61]

The powers and principalities also prefer that humans live out of relationship with *creation*. If we can regard God's Earth as

---

60. In *The Powers That Be: Theology for a New Millennium,* Walter Wink describes how historic Christianity also became an accomplice in the war-making enterprise. "For three centuries, no Christian author to our knowledge approved of Christian participation in battle . . . The early church theologian Tertullian (c.160–c.225) had pithy advice for soldiers who converted to Christianity: quit the army, or be martyred by the army for refusing to fight. When the emperor Constantine forbade pagan sacrifices by the army in 321 CE, most Christians apparently read this as removing a major objection to military service . . . When the Christian church began receiving preferential treatment by the very empire that it had so steadfastly opposed, war, which had once seemed so evil, now appeared to be a necessity for preserving the empire that protected the church . . . A fundamental transformation occurred when the church ceased being persecuted and became instead a persecutor" (p. 129).

61. Though a few occasions in human history have warranted warfare as a last resort necessary evil—that is, necessary, because of enormous failures on all sides, but nevertheless, evil—for the most part, as in Pharaoh's Egypt, the war industry, or the "military industrial complex" as President Eisenhower called it, generally serves as a mechanism of Cain's powers and principalities to wrest and sustain economic and political advantage.

One of the numerous bizarre examples of Cain's glorification of warfare is in Lintong District, China, at the site of the Terracotta Warriors mausoleum complex. Apparently, 2,200 years ago, China's first emperor, Qin Shi Huang Di, over a period of thirty years, coerced 700,000 workers to construct an "army" to do his bidding in the afterlife. Discovered by farmers in 1974, this multiple-acre complex consists of intricately carved statues positioned in trenchlike, underground corridors. The clay statuary includes 8,000 life-sized soldiers with different hairstyles, facial expressions, uniforms, and colored adornments, plus 130 chariots, 520 life-sized horses, and countless weapons. The human figures wield real bronze crossbows, swords, and lances. 40,000 arrowheads have been found. When Mr. Qin died in 210 BCE, this massive clay "army" (along with the 700,000 killed workers) was buried with him in regiment form. See "Terra-Cotta Warriors in Color" in *National Geographic* (June 2012): 74–87.

an object subservient to our species, it makes the messy details of doing business so much less messy. To the powers and principalities, "separate from, superior to, the reason for, and the rulers of" sounds just about right. We are the most important species, and this is as it should be. The rest of creation is meant to serve humankind. When confronted with information about the dire effects of our unsustainable practices for the future, the forces of Cain will often utter comments such as these:

- If whales, gorillas, and wetlands are so precious, why are they going extinct and not humans?[62]

- Doesn't my ability to destroy Abel show my superiority? If Abel is so great, why is he dead and not me?[63]

- I have money, land, possessions, and a strong military, so this will happen to other people, not to me or mine.

- Isn't a spectacular life of glory, however homicidal, brief, or suicidal, better than living as a mere gracious participant and wise steward of God's garden of life?

---

62. A T-shirt for a restaurant featuring barbeque meat boasts, "You did not fight your way to the top of the food chain to eat tofu and bean products."

63. Cain has been relentless in rising up to kill Abel wherever he is found. One can observe this in Cain's assault upon the so-called indigenous peoples of the world. Cain has been dogged and ruthless. The term "indigenous" is controversial, since the question of who got to a certain region first is sometimes unclear. Humans roam. And there have been back-and-forth skirmishes fought over access to water, forests, and land down through the ages. How far back does one go to determine first peoples? For me, the term "indigenous" refers to a worldview and way of life, a Leaver way of life. These peoples are not to be romanticized or demonized. They are neither saints nor demons. However, generally, over generations and generations, they have perceived their lives as with and within the community of life. They rarely saw themselves as separate from or superior to the land and its creatures. It is still this way among tiny remnants of nearly disseminated Leaver cultures around the globe today.

- I'll be dead by then, so I'm not going to worry.[64]

In addition to neighbor and creation, the powers and principalities also prefer that each of us remains disconnected from her or his own *inner spirit/soul/self*. Why? Because such living fosters emptiness. It generates hollowness and a purposeless existence. The powers and principalities understand that if we feel empty in the interior depths of our lives, we will want to fill that hunger with more "stuff." We will be willing and eager consumers. Former Latin American bishop Dom Helder Camera asks a humorous but haunting question in one of his poems: "How can one think, and feel, and be, when stuffed with jellied donuts?" The Cain/Taker cultures of the world produce jellied donuts in manifold forms, not just in the processed food industries. Like all junk foods, these are deficient in genuine nutrition. Thus, persons and cultures are left simultaneously fat and hungry, never satisfied, and craving (as one who is addicted) more and more.[65]

---

64. When I noticed one Saturday morning that the blueberries and grapes in the produce section of a local Tucson grocery store came from Argentina and Australia, I asked the assistant manager her thoughts. "People like fruit year round," she said. When I suggested that the shipping and pollution costs were significant, she said, "Yes, but it's what people want, and we can get you better prices from far away." When I replied, "But isn't serious damage being done to oceans and ecosystems?" she caught my drift and winked (we were about the same age), saying, "Well, you and I will be dead by the time it gets so bad." She was an ordinary person, and not evil in any way. She might even have been a religious person. But her comments indicated that, wittingly or unwittingly, she had surrendered to, and maybe even now championed, Cain's narrative. "Humans will probably destroy much of the Earth and there is not much we can do about it. But if we do destroy it, well, it was for us anyway." Without really thinking in these terms, she had succumbed to the aims of the powers and principalities.

65. In the George Lucas *Star Wars* films the grotesque Jabba the Hutt is described as "a great mobile tub of muscle and suet." (The 1987 Mel Brooks movie spoof *Spaceballs* refers to this corpulent creature as Pizza the Hutt.) Ravenous day and night, Jabba never has enough. His belly bellows and belches for more and more, even as such gluttony renders him less satisfied and less secure. This creature is the poster child for the powers and principalities, though through the miracle of advertising and even health clubs, Jabba's gluttony can be made to look slim and attractive.

And finally, the powers and principalities prefer that we remain disconnected from the *Creator*. God is the creator and owner of all life, including our own. "The Earth is the Lord's and the fullness thereof," proclaims the Psalmist (24:1), and "Your God reigns," declares the prophet Isaiah (52:7). But like mutineers on a ship at sea, the last thing we want to be reminded of is that neither the ship nor the sea nor the biosphere that holds it—not even our own lives—belong to us. We are not our own, and we do not have life in ourselves. It's the Creator's reign, for the benefit of the whole community life, that matters.

Major portions of our species now live out of relationship in a condition of "dis-ease" (Paul Tillich's term). This powerful state of "existential disrepair" makes us individually as well as collectively dangerous. No longer grounded, we chase flight. No longer fed, we consume artificial fillers, such as those churned out by the pervasive entertainment industry. No longer centered in truth, we become easy prey and even willing accomplices in the more mindless peregrinations and ominous distortions of reality.[66]

---

66. Another phrase that characterizes how the powers and principalities function is "group think." In my opinion, this term aptly describes the folly that drove the panic of 2002 and 2003, as the Bush-Cheney-Rumsfeld-Rice-Powell administration and the news media together orchestrated the false case for war upon the people of Iraq. The pressures to launch were enormous. Weapons makers needed to test products, soldiers needed to vent vitality, politicians were clamoring to appear patriotic, civilian industries had goods and services to market, universities had grant monies to access, and spy agencies had information to disseminate, much of which turned out to be exaggerated, if not fabricated. And the news media had endless opportunities begging to be exploited. The drumbeat for war proved irresistible. In such a milieu the denial of contrary evidence and easy twisting of facts started to feel normal to those involved. A distortive and inexorable force overtook the collective mind of many individuals and groups within the body politic.

Chapter 10
Problematic Christian Teachings
(Old Testament)

The powers and principalities ply their wares in a variety of realms including commercialism, government, military, and culture. They are ubiquitous, and they are deadly. But they are also present in Christian theology. In my view, several fundamental Christian teachings need to be investigated and challenged. I invite you to consider the following:

1. Dominion

Given the vastness and tremendous age of God's creation, the concept of dominion by humans, as I stated earlier, is as nonsensical as it is destructive. The varieties of creatures in

God's community of life don't need the human species to rule, manage, or develop them. The ecosystems of this Earth can do fine without us. Our species has a right to be here, just like fungi, elephants, and enzymes. But we don't have a right to rule.

So when the biblical storytellers in Genesis spoke of dominion, what were they getting at? They seem to be promoting a special role for humans. "God said to them [the human creatures], 'Fill the earth and subdue it; and have dominion over the fish of the sea and over the birds of the air and over every living thing that moves upon the earth'" (Genesis 1:28). On the surface the meaning appears to be clear. But are there shades of significance that a surface reading overlooks?

If by "dominion" the biblical storytellers meant exploitation and abuse, then this injunction is problematic. The damage done by equating human dominion with exploitation has been beyond measure, and further abuse is certain to lead to further destruction in God's beloved garden. The wider toll will even include our own species' spiritual, and eventual physical, deterioration. Exploitative and abusive living is unsustainable, and we should eliminate the idea that dominion means this for this reason alone.

Are there other possible meanings? As parents, my wife and I were in a relation of dominion with respect to our children while they were young. If this had meant ill treatment and abuse, then we should have been put in jail. But if dominion meant respecting, caring for, disciplining, protecting, and nurturing them so that they could grow, flourish, and become full persons blessing themselves, our family, and the whole community of life, then it is *tov*.

Also, my wife and I have been married for over three decades. In the marriage union, in a sense, she has dominion in relation to me and I have dominion in relation to her. Again, if this means mis-treatment and exploitation, then it is worthy of everyone's disdain. But if it means self-giving love, mutual respect, protection, and nurture so that the other may flourish and the marriage relationship may prosper and all members of the family and even the wider community may thrive, then it is *tov*.

Some Christians argue that the concept of dominion carries these meanings. Historically, a small portion of the Christian community has held this conviction. They have believed that the Creator gave dominion over the Earth to the species *Homo sapiens* as a sacred trust, and that we are commanded to be good and responsible stewards of this precious, living gift. This is certainly a better definition of "dominion" than the exploitative one. Still, what falls short for me about even this view is this: humans have been around for such a tiny fraction of time, for only 1/19,000th of the period that life has prospered on Earth. It seems presumptuous to say that Earth needs humans to rule it, to care for it, or even to protect it. Humans are not needed to "save the planet." The ecosystems and life-forms of this world can take care of and steward themselves just fine. Perhaps, however, the Earth would benefit if our species would learn how to *self*-regulate. Perhaps Earth would prosper again if we humans learned how to steward ourselves. If this is what is meant by Christian stewardship, then it may make sense.

What did the biblical storytellers mean when they used the term "dominion"? I do not know. I haven't found anyone else who knows, either. However, even despite the two examples of parenting and marriage, as well as the noble concept of creation-care, I am inclined to conclude that the concept of dominion is ultimately unsalvageable. There is no evidence in our brief 200,000-year history that our rule has been necessary, or that as it has regrettably emerged during short Cain's administration, beneficial. Considered individually and especially collectively, we are not the brightest kids on the block. Again, we may be capable of having dominion in relation to ourselves, but not anyone else. In my opinion, the Church would do well to retire this word from its vocabulary.

2. Original Sin

Along with dominion, the doctrine of original sin is equally problematic. Although this teaching is now deeply embedded in the psyche of Western civilization and in Western Christianity, it is interesting to note that original sin is stressed neither in Judaism nor in Eastern Orthodox Christianity. Judaism stresses more the rainbow promise at the end of the Noah story as a sign of full restoration from the effects of Adam and Eve's sin. "The Lord said, 'I set my bow in the cloud, and it shall be a sign of the covenant between me and the earth'" (Genesis 9:13). For its part, Eastern Orthodox Christianity clings more to the notion of "original blessing." This view says that while sin certainly exists and needs to be resisted, creation and humanity are fundamentally *tov*.[67] The same is true in much of African spirituality. It is Western Christianity that has strained over original sin.

The doctrine of original sin argues that humanity is fallen, and therefore every human born is inevitably at odds with God, creation, our neighbors, and with our own inner spirit/souls/selves. It is our nature, after all; we are "sin-full." If we are ruining the planet, what's the big surprise? It may be tragic, but why would anyone expect otherwise? So Christians, lay and clergy, look down at their feet, and mutter sighing phrases such as,

- "What can we do? It's human nature."

- "If we could just rid ourselves of human nature . . . but I don't see this happening anytime soon." (Chuckle, chuckle.)

- "Perhaps God will intervene and fix things before the situation gets too bad."

---

67.   See Matthew Fox, *Original Blessing: A Primer in Creation Spirituality*.

- "Nothing will change unless the rest of the world becomes Christian like us."

In truth, we Christians are doing our full share of the harm. Christians work in, and are responsible for decisions in, all the major commercial, academic, and governmental industries of the world. There is almost no area where we are not presently making an impact. And just as troubling, Christians seem to exhibit an addiction to consumerism and pollution equal to those with other lifestyles and religions. While many Christians do admirable charity work to clean up humanity's messes *after* the fact, along with other groups in society who are also charitable, on the front end, we do as much damage as anyone.

There is also a secular version of the notion of original sin, which our culture has readily assimilated. One could see this exhibited vividly during the 2008–2011 global financial meltdown. Television networks interviewed many "experts" in an attempt to pinpoint the reasons for the crisis. It was telling to observe that whenever the interviewer posited "greed" as the driving force of the problem, most contestants in the debate perfunctorily sighed, "Oh, that's just human nature," and then proceeded on to the next topic. Greed was considered a given: "It's how we are wired, and it is naive to expect otherwise, so let's just move on." Such thinking becomes not only a self-fulfilling prophecy, but also an opportunistic justification for continued harmful decisions and behaviors.

So my argument is this: sin, greed, and I-centeredness are not the sum total of who we are. They are not "our nature," but rather options "within our nature," along with generosity, community, courage, and respect. We are not fated to go the way of Takerism. In fact, for the first two hundred thousand years of our species' existence, Cain's narrative was not dominant. This aberration occurred, certainly. But when it did, it did so only occasionally and in isolated locations. It was contained by Earth's checks and balances. In a sense, this is good news. It is cause for a measure of hopefulness. It means that we are not robotically locked into a destiny dominated by homicidal, and potentially suicidal, megaconduct. It also means that the biblical Fall stories in Genesis 3 and following, although not describing something called original sin, are actually important Abel stories that warn us about the destructiveness of human-centered thinking and the accompanying behaviors that trample God's world.[68]

In summary, my view is that the concept of dominion is problematic and needs to be discarded. It thrusts much of humanity in a direction contrary to God's 13.7 billion year primary mission—the evolving story of life—and contrary to God's recently inaugurated (in the past several thousand years) secondary mission of trying to heal humans and bring us back into the Creator's household with and within the community of life under the permeating reign of God—that is, into God's primary mission.[69]

---

68.   Does Abel engage in sin, greed, and I-centeredness? Of course. Abel goes off the mark, too. But because Abel lives in "relationship" with the community of life, with the ancient wisdom of his species' longer history, with his own inner spirit/soul/self, and with the Creator, rather than in a recently chosen state of disconnectedness like Cain, Abel's sins are amendable.

69.   I do not advocate a return to the past, or that we all become hunter-gatherers like our ancestors. The Earth could not endure 7 billion hunter-gathers. And much of modern life is good and wholesome, including many medical advances, transportation and communications, and even space exploration, in my opinion. We cannot, nor should we, try to go back to former times. I do advocate, however, that we return to the *present*—to relationship with Creator, neighbor, creation, and inner spirit today. Humanity is out of touch. We are living and consuming as though Earth's human population is 1 billion rather than 7 billion. We have adopted Cain's narrative. We are not fitting in. Indeed, we take pride in not fitting in. This chosen narrative—human exceptionalism, anthropo-narcissism, "diva" theology—is blinding us from being responsible participants in the Creator's household.

I also believe that the church's teachings on original sin have incorrectly been associated with Genesis 3 and following. These parables are not talking about the same concepts that would later become Church doctrines. Rather, the parables in Genesis 3 and following reflect a troubling divergence from Abel living that occurred in history, and that the storytellers were experiencing in their locale 3,000 to 4,000 years ago. This megashift had begun in other parts of the world only several thousand years earlier, and was now at their doorstep at the time of their writing.[70]

I believe both the religious and secular versions of original sin lie in opposition to God's story of life and God's story of Jesus. In contrast to the notion of dominion, however, I'm not yet convinced this doctrine needs to be totally jettisoned. My Lutheran upbringing probably is a factor in my hesitation. After all, the concept of original sin provides us with a way to appreciate the gross magnitude of Cain's sorry administration. It shows us the ugliness of Cain's folly. However, it needs reinterpretation, especially if it implies that humans are locked in an inevitable pathway of destruction (of others, the Earth, and of ourselves), endless greed, conflict with our neighbors, and spiritual emptiness. It needs reinterpretation if it implies that faith in Jesus fixes these deficiencies for us without our need to turn around from Cain's ways and physically come with the risen Jesus into restored relationships. And it needs reinterpretation in order that it might become a fresh and reconsidered doctrine that blesses God's world, blesses the community of life, and blesses our species.

---

70. If Genesis 2 and following appeared in written form around 900 BCE, it is also quite possible that these stories circulated as oral traditions for several decades or even centuries prior. Hence, 3,000 to 4,000 years.

Chapter 11
Problematic Christian Teachings
(New Testament)

There are also problematic Christian teachings that find their beginnings in the New Testament. These teachings have become inflated throughout Christian history, and in their present form distort renderings of God's story of life and God's story of Jesus. What follows are two fundamentals that, in my view, need to be disassembled.

1. Atonement theories

There are several theories of atonement that people draw from the Bible that focus on a day Christians call Good Friday. These theories attempt to answer questions such as the following: What does the cross mean? Why did Jesus die? Did his passion and death accomplish something of Earthly significance? Of cosmic significance? Did a transaction take place between God and humanity? Between God and the creation? Various atonement theories have been developed over the centuries to address such questions. What follows is a brief explanation of several of them, along with a suggestion of why I think they should be set aside.

- **Sacrificial theory of atonement.** This theory considers Jesus as the greatest of all sacrifices. The "Lamb of God who takes away the sin of the world" gave his life as a slaughtered sacrifice, so that "once and for all" God's need and desire to be sacrificed to would be forever satisfied. Adherents say, "Jesus died for me." What they mean is that the blood/death of Jesus took care of what was wrong between God and humanity. "It's all about the blood" goes the refrain. Rob Bell, in his book *Love Wins: A Book about Heaven, Hell, and the Fate of Every Person Who Ever Lived*, writes about the cross as "the end of the sacrificial system . . . a broken relationship that's been reconciled . . . a guilty defendant who's been set free . . . a battle that's been won . . . the redeeming of something that was lost."[71]

  According to this theory, the crucifixion of Jesus marks the termination of a divinely-installed sacrificial system. God's status as Deity required—for a time—the sacrificial slaying of animals or humans, and for a time God found such practices laudable demonstrations of faithfulness and obedience. The foundational Old Testament story for this way of thinking is in Genesis 22. This episode concerns

---

71.   San Francisco: HarperOne, 127ff.

the near-murder of a boy named Isaac by his dad, Abraham. In the narrative, the storytellers have God command Abraham to kill and burn the only child he and his wife Sarah have conceived together as a test of faith. Abraham sneaks the boy away from his mother and brings him up Mount Moriah.[72] There, he sets up an altar, gathers firewood, and prepares to carry out the proscribed deed. Just as Abraham is about to stab the boy to death, an angel of the LORD stops him, saying, "Do not lay your hand on the boy or do anything to him; for now I know that you fear God, since you have not withheld your son, your only son, from me" (Genesis 22:12). At the last moment, the LORD provides a ram that had been caught by its horns in the bushes, which Abraham slays and cooks. This animal becomes a stand-in blood/burnt offering for what Abraham was willing to make of his child. "So Abraham called that place 'The LORD will provide'; and it is said to this day, 'on the mount of the LORD it shall be provided'" (Genesis 22:14). As this is applied to the Jesus narrative, Jesus becomes the stand-in blood offering that the Deity in his mercy provides, thereby satisfying the requirement of blood, as well as ending the need to ever do it again. As the theory goes, Jesus satisfied God's need for a sacrifice once and for all, and the benefits of salvation go to those who believe that God and Jesus did this for them.

---

72. One has to wonder how this bizarre and clandestine episode affected the marriage of Sarah and Abraham. Would a wife ever trust her husband again? How did this play out in the family system? Might this incident have had something to do with the extreme dysfunction (cheating, lying, murder, incest, revenge, selling a brother into slavery) of their grandson Jacob and his family years later?

What, if anything, is wrong with this doctrine? Though the Old Testament writers certainly present the sacrificial system as something God instituted, and other cultures and religions have practiced sacrificial rituals also, nevertheless, in my view, the notion that God *ever* got a kick out of sacrifices is at best a Cain/Taker invention. At worst, it is a scheme to try to manipulate God. When Christians portray Jesus' death on the cross as a requirement to satisfy God by means of a sacrifice, or to pay a penalty to God for human sins committed against God, neighbor, creation, and inner spirit by means of a sacrifice, Christian theology gets pulled into this system. Unless I'm missing something here and something magical going on, how can a burnt grain or slaughtered animal or a person's carcass have the power to restore relationship, which is God's goal? A sacrifice does not restore relationships.[73]

- **Substitution theory of atonement.** This scenario portrays a deity who seethes over human sin. God's anger/wrath has built up and must be expelled somewhere. God's need for retributive justice must be satisfied, which requires that offenders be

---

73. In the Bible, animal sacrifices were limited to cattle, sheep, goats, doves, and pigeons. They had to be both male and unblemished, criteria that displayed a deep cultural prejudice against females and against handicapped or scarred creatures, including humans. Other sacrificial articles included wheat, barley, olive oil, wine, and frankincense. Sacrifice became an act of worship for many. That said, there are also occasions in the Bible when this view is countered. From the prophet Amos we hear the LORD declare, "I hate, I despise your festivals, and I take no delight in your solemn assemblies. Even though you offer me your burnt offerings and grain offerings, I will not accept them; and the offering of well-being of your fatted animals I will not look upon . . . But let justice roll down like waters, and righteousness like an everflowing stream" (Amos 5:21–22, 24). Even the biblical narrative is torn about this bizarre ritual. (See also Micah 6:6–8).

punished. However, in grace, God decides not to punish humanity for their transgressions. Instead, God provides a substitute. Jesus of Nazareth becomes that substitutionary lamb upon whom the Deity can vent divine rage. The venting occurs, Jesus dies, and God feels relief. Now, those who believe in Jesus can transfer God's anger toward them onto Jesus, the vicarious scapegoat, sparing them from eternal punishment. Adherents say, "Jesus died for me." This means that Jesus gave his life to satisfy not only God's anger, but also God's cosmic demand for retributive justice.[74] Adherents say, "My sins deserve God's punishment, but Jesus took the hit in my place. If I believe this, I'll be saved. I should be grateful, live a good life, and tell others that this is the way to be spared from God's wrath."

What, if anything, is wrong with this doctrine? I see it as portraying God as powerless to control God's own rage. Also, it claims that God's justice requires punishment. What is paramount in this scenario is that retribution be exacted, whether on to the guilty person, on to a bad person who is guilty of a different crime, or even on to an innocent bystander. God's need for retributive justice is utmost, and must be satisfied. I suggest that this popular understanding of God's justice represents the mind and heart of Cain rather than the mind and heart of the Creator or Abel of Nazareth.

---

74. Retributive justice, which can be found in the Bible, is a much different form of justice than the deeper biblical notion of distributive justice, which is concerned that all have enough and none too much, and restorative justice, which seeks to reconcile strangers, outcasts, aliens, and enemies.

- **Ransom theory of atonement.** Here, Satan has kidnapped humanity from God's kingdom. God pays a ransom (Jesus' slain life) to get humanity back. Adherents say, "Jesus died for me." By this they mean, "I was kidnapped; the kidnapper demanded a million dollar ransom (Jesus' death); God came up with the ransom payment, put it in a briefcase (the grave), and gave it to Satan in exchange for me. See how much Jesus loved me. I am grateful to be freed and will live an indebted life and tell others that Jesus will pay their ransom costs, too."

  What, if anything, is wrong with this doctrine? For this theory to be credible, one would have to imagine a Creator who would engage in such deal making with a Satan figure. In my opinion, this is too contradictory to the persistent biblical assertion and celebration of the reign of God.

- **Supersufferer theory of atonement.** This theory argues that God was so impressed with the heroic x-rated sufferings of Jesus and the devotion to God that such willingness to suffer demonstrated, that God decided to forgive everyone who believes in this *Braveheart* sufferer. This is the basic theology of Mel Gibson's 2005 film, *The Passion of the Christ*. Walter Wink, in *The Powers That Be*, refers to this as the "myth of redemptive violence," as he offers a brilliant description of how we are schooled in this myth from early childhood onward. In this myth, terrible violent things need to happen in order to produce goodness. Life is combat, violence saves, suffering is required, and war brings peace.

What, if anything, is wrong with this doctrine? Redemptive suffering portrays God as either masochistic or sadistic, depending on how one understands Jesus. It can also glorify unjust suffering, and in a curious way even make war, slavery, famine, or abuse seem noble. Suffering is my God-given burden, and God will reward me if I endure it. Some slaveholders in the American South are said to have encouraged the acceptance of such ideas by their slaves. "It is your 'cross to bear.'" Some priests and pastors have even counseled women to stay with abusive husbands because "it will make you a stronger person." Restoration and good sometimes follow seasons of suffering. And I recognize that mild forms of suffering have made me a stronger person in some ways. But to say that suffering was necessary for good to occur is mistaken. Embracing such a view becomes a familial, cultural, or nationalistic defense mechanism that enables groups and individuals to block their eyes and hearts from witnessing the suffering of others, or doing anything to alleviate it. This explains how we can indulge in guiltless plentitude while others go without, or assuage the extreme wastefulness and grief of pollution or warfare so easily. We just make heroes/martyrs out of those who suffer. Again, this seems to be the theological/emotional affect that Mel Gibson's movie was trying to stimulate.

These atonement theories pervade much of Christian theology and much of Cain's culture. Even though some justification for all of them can be found in the Christian scriptures, I am among those who believe they are deficient in what they communicate about the meaning of God's primary and secondary missions. The problem is they all require payoffs, and in some cases, retribution, which is contrary to the notion of a forgiving God. The sacrificial and substitutionary systems assert that someone must die in order for God's wrath to be placated. The blood, the death, the carcass are all obligatory to make God happy. In the ransom theory a Satan figure gets the payoff. And in the supersufferer idea the suffering itself becomes the payment. It is recompense to make things right.[75]

But if such traditional theories of the atonement fall short, portraying a terribly diminutive God, as I believe they do, what, then, are Jesus' life and crucifixion really about? Who was—who is—this woodworker from Nazareth? Why did he live? Why then? What is the significance of the incarnation (enflesh-ment)? Why did Jesus behave so contrary to the powers and principalities of culture, country, and religion? What do his teachings, miracles, and exorcisms accomplish? What happened on the cross? What happened at the resurrection? Volumes have been written on these questions. What follows is my attempt at a response in light of this new framing.

In my view, the Jesus event (including his birth, servant ministry, challenge of the powers and principalities, alternative way of living, crucifixion, death, and counterintuitive resurrec-tion) demonstrates in the clearest possible way God's prefer-ence for the fragrant offerings of Abel, that is, for Abel's way of Leaver living. It proclaims God's profound desire for wayward

---

75.   Again, Walter Wink's book, *The Powers That Be: Theology for a New Millennium,* is an excellent resource on the fallacies of all these atonement theories.

humanity to be healed and to rejoin the community of life, so that the world may be saved from Cain's assault. Furthermore, it is a harsh reminder that living the Abel way of life, which in the context of Cain's rebellion can be seen as a "cross life," will usually trigger violent reactivity from the powers and principalities of Cain. Takers will always battle preemptively or in response to perceived threat in order to preserve their way. Cain will always assemble the justification needed to rise up and kill Abel. However, even if persecutions come our way, we are not to despair. Why? Because not only is Abel's way abounding in honor and goodness, it is also ultimately immune to Cain's final sedition. "Neither death . . . nor principalities . . . nor powers . . . nor anything else in all creation, will be able to separate us from the love of God in Christ Jesus our Lord" (Romans 8:37–39).

To me, the cross event is important because the crucified Abel of Nazareth stands as *mirror* and *window*. As *mirror*, his death reflects back to me the true nature of Takerism. What does my Takerism look like? It looks like the Creator's goodness in human form and in living color rejected and crucified by me and mine. That's its ugliness. That's the rub. And lest I think my Taker ways are not that big of deal, or that they can be covered up or rationalized away, the cross of Jesus forces sin's display in all of its misshapen splendor.

Jesus' death is also *window*. Through the window of the outstretched arms of the hanging Abel Christ, our species is granted a holy glimpse into the broken heart of God, and into the immense essence of God's love for the cosmos, including humans, including Abel, and, surprisingly, including Cain. This love has an enormity of grace that surpasses all understanding. It forgives. It challenges. It is self-sacrificing. It is expansive, beguiling, and life empowering. The cross event boldly proclaims the good news, "God loves this world; God even loves the lost species that amusingly calls itself *Homo sapiens sapiens* (wise, wise one); and God will not give up."

In Galilee, at the beginning of his ministry, Jesus lived the creative and verdant ways of Abel. In Jerusalem, toward the end, Jesus experienced the barren forsakenness of the ways of Cain. Cain's armed reaction to God's story of Jesus was the same as Cain's armed reaction to God's story of life: "Away with him. Away with him. Crucify him" (John 19:15). In contrast, God's disarming response to Cain's pattern of terror was not only "Put away your sword; for all who take the sword will perish [spiritually, as well as emotionally, physically, and culturally] by the sword" (Matthew 26:52), and "Father, forgive them, for they know not what they do" (Luke 23:34), but also, and most importantly, resurrection. After deceasing into real death, Jesus was raised from the dead into real and eternal life. Because of this resurrection, Jesus is alive today. And because he is alive today, his embodied message continues to be as it has been for two thousand years, "*Homo sapiens,* God forgives you; repent, and follow me."

This is important. Another way to say it is this: Jesus was not sent by God to *die* a "cross death"—or any other kind of death. His death was certainly inevitable, as death is for all mortal creatures, including humans. And his alternative way of living predictably produced spasms of violent reactivity in Cain. But Jesus did not come with the objective of dying. Rather, Jesus came to live. He was ordained by God to live a cross *life*. He was ordained to live as God intends all creatures, including humans, to live.

Much of Christian theology has maintained the view that it was necessary for Jesus to die on the cross—that his spilt blood and dead carcass were required by God in order for God to accomplish his plan to save humanity. Much of Christianity has come to see the crucifixion as the core purpose to Jesus' Earthly existence. Both the Apostles' Creed and Nicene Creed foster this view by leaping immediately from the birth of Jesus ("born of the virgin Mary") to his final week ("suffered under

Pontius Pilate, was crucified, died, and was buried"). They skip the in-between years. But what about his teachings, close encounters with the lilies of the fields and birds of the air, and resolute conflicts with spiritual and human powers and principalities? What about the healings, his refusal to embrace violence and war as a way to solve problems, and his love for those considered strange, outcast, alien, and even enemies? The creeds imply that Jesus was born . . . and then he died, and that this is what is important. This is the view that I question.[76]

In its place, I suggest that Jesus did not have to die a cross death—which would somehow satisfy God's presumed need to be sacrificed to, gratify God's alleged requirement of retribution, placate Satan's demand for a ransom payment, or attend to God's reputed requisite that suffering must occur before good can come. Rather, what was eminently necessary was that Jesus came (comes) to live.

Although living an Abel life, which can be called a cross life under Cain's dominion, often causes a reaction of rejection, suffering, and even death, as it did for Jesus, it is this cross life that is salvific. The way Jesus lived, the way he lives today, and his call for us to receive forgiveness, turn around (repent), and follow him into restored relationship is the way home for our species back into the Creator's house with and within the community of life under the permeating reign of God. It is the way of healing. It is "the resurrection and the life" (John 11:25).

But what about forgiveness? Didn't the death of Jesus bring about a new reality in the world, namely forgiveness? We forget that the blessing of forgiveness existed long before Jesus was born. He announced it, certainly, and made it clearer,

---

76. It should also be noted that the creeds hop from "I believe in God the Father Almighty, maker of heaven and earth" to "I believe in Jesus Christ his only son our Lord." But what about the 13.7 billion years of God's activity and care in between these two events? The creeds not only diminish Jesus' ministry in my view, they also diminish the vastness and ancient splendor of the Creator's creative reign.

and pointedly broke through cultural and religious barriers to make sure outcasts and more vulnerable sinners knew it was for them, too. But Jesus didn't invent God's forgiveness. Jesus didn't need to die for forgiveness to occur. The cross no doubt made it more painfully evident and vivid to us why we need to be forgiven, but the cross didn't bring some new thing that God finally decided to introduce to the universe after 13.7 billion years of evolving history.

Today, the risen Christ embodies God's long-standing forgiveness, along with the call/invitation/command to repent, and the call to follow Jesus into restored relationship with neighbors, creation, inner spirit, and with God. This "way, truth, and life" (John 14:6) is wherein the workings of salvation transpire, conspire, and inspire. This way is sometimes accompanied with joy and glorious relief. At other times, the restoration is worked out "with fear and trembling" (Philippians 2:12). But in these ways of salvation the *powers* of sin and death are overcome. Not sin, but the power of sin. Not natural death, which is part of God's evolving garden of life, but perishing death, which is separation from the community of life, from ourselves, and from God.

The historic theories of the atonement need to be set aside, in my view. They make more out of the cross death of Jesus than is there, and they deflect us from what is necessary for healing to begin. The world doesn't need more Christians who sing praises to Jesus' fatality. Rather, it needs more of us to go with Jesus in the cross life he lives today. The execution of Jesus was not necessary in the sense that God required it. Jesus' death was not the main thing. But it happened, and God answered it with resurrection. Receiving forgiveness, turning one hundred eighty degrees away from Cain's murderous folly, and following Jesus into repaired relationship with creation, neighbors, self, and the Creator is the way, truth, and life. It is the way of true "at-one-ment," and it is for today. "See, now is the acceptable time; see now is the day of salvation" (2 Corinthians 6:2b).

So the struggle goes on. Death did not stop Jesus. Cain's powers and principalities are not as strong as they seem. They do not contain life and they are not the means to life. Indeed, these forces are perishing and these forces are doomed. It is the meek of the world, Jesus and his Abel followers as well as the whole community of life, who "will inherit the Earth" (Matthew 5:5) and more.

2. Eschatology

Along with the church's teachings on dominion, original sin, and atonement, a final impediment within historic and contemporary Christianity has to do with eschatology, or "end times." In Cain's version of Christianity, whether the notion was intended from the beginning or came after the Fall, Earth's ending (some even think the cosmos's ending) is central to God's divine plan. God wishes to destroy the world and bring into existence a new heaven and a new universe, including a new Earth. When following this line of thinking, it can become easy to be unconcerned about things like human overpopulation, pollution, and plummeting water tables—as many Christians are. Why worry about human-caused climate change, depleted soils, or the extinction of other species? It is all passing away anyway. God is bringing a new creation. The old is passing away. A replacement is coming. Such is the thinking of Cain and the thinking of much of popular Christianity.[77]

But it is not just these views that are harmful. My own tradition, so-called progressive Christianity, is also problematic. While our tradition doesn't believe God plans to destroy

---

77. A portion of those who hold this view might promote recycling and antilittering efforts. But this is primarily for the benefit of *Homo sapiens,* so that we can at least keep the Earth somewhat aesthetically pleasant and verdant until God destroys it and takes us someplace else.

the Earth—it maintains that God instead intends to fulfill it—it also embraces the underlying presumption that God's creation is *presently* partial (some even think deficient), and that the whole creation needs to be overhauled. We are encouraged to "lean into the future" toward a glorious and imminent fulfillment, an omega point up ahead toward which all creation is being pulled on its way to final consummation and glory.

I see at least four problems with this theology. First, such thinking can make one dissatisfied with God's garden. It can feed a discontent with what the Creator calls good. Second, while it is true that those parts of God's Earth that have been ruined by Cain's misbehavior certainly need repairing—and there are many—it is also true that the whole Earth does not need redeeming; and certainly not the whole cosmos. The evolving and ever-changing creation is *tov* in God's eyes: very good. To suggest that the misbehavior of one species out of twenty million on Earth, on a tiny speck of a planet in one minuscule arm of an average galaxy, that resides in the midst of trillions and trillions of solar systems throughout billions and billions of galaxies, to suggest that this species brought about the Fall of the cosmos, is not only pretentious, but is also silly. Only a creature that presumes itself to be primary would think this. But in truth, it is only our species that needs redeeming. It is only the species *Homo sapiens* that is at war with all the Creator holds dear, that needs to find its way home again.

Third, this theology quickly becomes just another addiction, this time to the future (or to the novel, or newfangled, or to whatever is other than what we have). It turns our eyes and hearts to another place and time. It becomes a diversion from the call/invitation/command to follow the risen Christ into restored relationship with what is right in front of us this moment, namely our neighbors, the wider community of life, our inner spirits, and the Creator.

Finally, this theology can foster the notion that this Earth is not humanity's true home. Rather, heaven is. Earth may be for lesser creatures, but it is not a true habitat for humanity. We are going someplace else, somewhere new and improved. I believe in heaven, as I addressed in chapter 8. However, humanity's true home now is with the rest of the community of life in the Creator's household on Earth. If we can't be faithful/responsible/ethical with and within the community of life here, how will we be faithful/responsible/ethical with and within the community of life in heaven? Our attempts to presume otherwise only contribute to our current course of unsustainable and unfaithful living.

Ironically, as with the doctrine of original sin, Christian views of eschatology also have a secular counterpart, especially among younger generations. I do not know the percentages, but a significant portion of the American public seems to buy into the notion that if humans make the Earth unlivable, we will simply fly away and colonize other planets. Many people think *Star Trek* is our future. This notion is naïve for several reasons. First, there is no planet or moon in our solar system that is habitable for humans, so we would need to create a biosphere. But even if we could one day develop a biosphere on another planet amendable to photosynthesis and therefore capable of sustaining even a handful of people, the costs for such an undertaking would be astronomical in every category, including mineral resources, fuel, time, pollution, and money.

What if we could find a habitable planet similar to Earth in another solar system outside of our own? Could we travel there? How big a factor is distance? Would such star hopping be possible? To put this in perspective, we might recall that it took three days for our astronauts to travel to the moon. They traveled an impressive distance of 240,000 miles in 72 hours. So at these speeds, how long would it take for a spaceship to fly to our nearest solar system, *Proxima Centuri*? This star is 4.2 light years, or 24 trillion miles away from Earth. The answer is 800,000 *years*. What if scientists someday were to develop rockets capable of propelling us eight times the current velocity limits, or even eighty times faster? It would still take 100,000 years or 10,000 years, respectively, to get to the *nearest* solar system to ours—one way. Add to this the reality that there are not enough financial, mineral, and fuel resources on planet Earth to send even one spaceship. And of course the overwhelming trauma of such an ordeal would take us far beyond the physical limits of our human bodies. We would not physically survive even a fraction of such a trip.

Some will argue that "all things are possible" with technology. One hundred and fifty years ago no one dreamed that humans would one day fly in airplanes, let alone travel to the moon. Sixty years ago, one computer took up the space of a whole room and employed cumbersome vacuum tubes to feed, store, and process data. Today, one laptop can do the work of hundreds of those computers. These technological marvels are real and significant. Certainly, human ingenuity is often impressive. The Internet itself has only existed since the early 1990s, and who knows what the future holds? However, even if such space travel could one day come about in theory, the technological advancements required for humans to make travel outside of our solar system a reality is hundreds or thousands of years into the future. Given our population and pollution trends, does it seem feasible that we can wait this long to see if Cain's rationale for making the Earth unlivable is sane?

I have suggested that the powers and principalities are in opposition to God's story of life and God's story of Jesus. I have also suggested that certain fundamental Christian concepts such as dominion, original sin, traditional theories of atonement, and eschatology are equally problematic. They divert us from what is important. I want next to talk about sustainable living, and then conclude with a section about hope and action.

PART V

Towards Sustainable Living: Is There Hope?

"A truly good book teaches me better than to read it.
I must soon lay it down, and commence living on its hint.
What I began by reading, I must finish by acting."

—Henry David Thoreau

Chapter 12
What is Sustainable Living?

Cain's narrative of Takerism has gained traction only in the last 9,000 to 5,000 years. It was either nonexistent or disarmed and contained during most of the first 200,000 years of human history. Currently, however, it is the dominating manifestation and domineering manifesto of our species. Very few human cultures today value or practice living with and within the community of life. And most prefer and practice a human-centered worldview and existence. All this leads to the number-one problem of our time, namely sustainability. Several issues stand out.

In August 2009, a CBS *60 Minutes* segment called "The Wasteland" reported that U.S. citizens throw away 130,000 computers per day. This is more than forty-seven million computers trashed each year. To replace a broken machine is one thing. But to be addicted to faster and faster and more and more creates uncalled for and preventable garbage. And such planned obsolescence is intentionally built into our economic system. The program also examined the recycling industry and found much that was disconcerting. Computers and monitors that are turned in for recycling are often sold from one company to another, and then to another, with minimal or no regulation. Many machines end up being dismantled by children in poor nations, with deadly toxins such as lead, mercury, chromium, and polyvinyl chlorides contaminating their fingernails and lungs, and their communities' soils and water systems.

Shopping malls are also indicative of the problem and attending dilemmas. In the average shopping mall, what percentage of the products sold are wholesome and necessary? What percentage is wasteful and waste producing? Bringing these goods and services to market provides jobs, certainly. This is the dilemma. But is the product itself complementary to God's primary and secondary missions? What are the long-term effects of many products? What footprint is being left behind during the mining, manufacturing, and disposing phases of a product's lifetime? How do we find wise leaders and wise business people to help us develop a thriving and sustainable Abel/Leaver economy, rather than help us stay the present course of unsustainability. Is this possible? I don't know.

Human population growth is also a significant factor. It took 200,000 years for the human global population to reach 1.5 billion. This occurred in 1901, the year Teddy Roosevelt assumed the presidency after William McKinley was assassinated. By the time John Kennedy became president sixty years later, the population had doubled to 3 billion. In 2012, fifty-one years later, it has more than doubled to over 7 billion. Future trends are ominous. Cautious population projections show an increase to 10 or 11 billion by 2050, and 14 or 15 billion by the end of this century. One wonders whether the Earth can endure this many of our species. Moreover, can we endure this many of ourselves?

Perhaps we are tempted to point to the high birth rates in poorer nations as the culprit of world population growth. The northern African country of Niger has the highest birth rate in the world at 48.8 per 1,000 (2009 statistic). However, consider this: the average person in the United States consumes and pollutes eight times the world's average. Thus, a four-person household in the United States actually causes annual damage equivalent to a thirty-two-person household in an average country, and damage equivalent to a sixty-four-person household in a poor country. If the current population of the United States is over 300 million, our nation's natural resource usage and negative ecological impact is equivalent to a population of over 2.4 billion.[78]

Furthermore, modern food production costs in rich nations are surprisingly high in terms of fossil fuel usage. Richard Heinberg writes,

> Modern industrial agriculture has become energy-intensive in every respect. Tractors and other farm machinery burn diesel fuel or gasoline; nitrogen fertilizers are produced from natural gas; pesticides and herbicides are synthesized from oil; seeds, chemicals, and crops are transported long distances by truck; and foods are often

---

78. Another way to measure this is that the United States has 5 percent of the world's population but uses 40 percent of the world's renewable resources and causes 40 percent of the world's pollution. If we and similar nations and cultures can decide to become more responsible, we have the potential to affect substantial reductions in our species' negative impact. Ironically, this shows that rich countries really do have a lot of power to do good.

It is also sobering to observe that both China and India (representing 37 percent of the world's population) are taking up the enticement to consume and pollute like the United States and other wealthy nations. Given our history, we probably don't have either the ethical credibility or power to reproach their quest, but again, we can make steps in self-regulating our own values and behaviors.

cooked with natural gas and packaged in oil-derived plastics before reaching the consumer. If food-production efficiency is measured by the ratio between the amount of energy input required to produce a given amount of food and the energy contained in that food, then industrial agriculture is by far the least efficient form of food production ever practiced.[79]

Industrial agriculturists often argue that destructive, unsustainable farming methods are necessary in order to produce enough food to feed the poor. They reason that we can't possibly grow sufficient quantities if farmers are committed to growing quality and nutritious food, to preserving water and soil ecosystems, to treating animals with respect, and to providing fair wages for workers. However, the reality may be more straightforward. Perhaps there is plenty of food in the world to feed the poor—but not the rich. People in wealthy nations consume multiple times their share, producing a groaning not only of God's creation, but also of their bodies, psyches, and spirits.

I have given just a small sampling of the many troubling areas on the horizon. We could also discuss the plummeting water tables, melting ice caps, desertification, coral reef and fish population diminishment, accumulating toxic trash, the loading of chemical stressors into our bodies, or air and water pollution[80]—all because of Cain's decision to embrace the ways of Takerism.

So what is the challenge before us? What must we accomplish in order to change direction and be on a better pathway?

---

79. Richard Heinberg, *The Party's Over: Oil, War, and the Fate of Industrial Societies,* 193.

80. In the northern Pacific Ocean there is today a great garbage patch of plastic soup comprised of tons and tons of waste and debris. This floating expanse of flotsam covers an area the size of the continental United States. One-fifth of the junk is thrown off of ships and oil platforms. The rest comes from industrial and household waste on land. This is after most of the refuse has already littered the ecosystems on the ocean floor.

Consider figure 3 as we think about these questions.

Figure 3

10	Worst
9	**Green**
8	**Non-sustainable living**
7	
6	
5	
4	
3	**Sustainable living**
2	
1	Pristine, *BWCA*

In the above chart the number ten on the scale refers to a way of life that is so egregious that it fouls oceans, alters climate, and triggers the extinction of entire species. A kind of living that ranks as a ten involves human behavior at its worst. At the other end of the spectrum is number one, associated with pristine living. One example of such living is the *Boundary Waters Canoe Area* in northern Minnesota, where the guidelines to preserving this space represent pristine living. The ethic for this wilderness reserve is to leave no toxic footprint: zero. "Take nothing out; leave nothing behind." That's the motto.

Obviously, it is unlikely that ours, or any species, will ever sustain the kind of living that would rank at number one, though perhaps we might approach it on wilderness canoe trips. Nor need we necessarily try. The goal, rather, is to get to number five. The goal is to cross the line from the domain of unsustainable barrenness into the world of sustainable and regenerative prosperity.

How do we do this? The current "green revolution" (which involves upgrading light bulbs, installing solar panels, recycling, organic gardening, composting, water harvesting, improving insulations, buying cars with better gas mileage, etc.) has the potential to get us to number nine in my view. This is a good thing and we should definitely do it—let's not be totally foolish. However, number-nine living is not adequate. It is still on the side of unsustainability. The challenge is to get to number five.

How do we do this, especially if the efforts of the green revolution are not sufficient? The thesis of this book is that the dominant narrative of our species, human exceptionalism, is the subliminal and overriding problem. My thesis is that this ideology supersedes all else in steeling and steering humanity's crushing boot print upon God's Earth. This saboteur is the one above all others. This thesis may sound trivial at first hearing. What could possibly be so important about a mere narrative? But this is my argument. As long as the dominant cultures of humanity continue to embrace Cain/Takerism's worldview with their minds, institutions, industries, and cultural myths, this will continue to be the defining narrative of our species. We will continue to enact it, because this is what humans do; we enact narratives. An individual's or family's *story* shapes much of how that family system unfolds. The founding *narrative* of a culture or nation shapes the worldview, values, and destiny of that culture or nation. Even a species' *myth*—of how it came to be, its place in relation to other species, its relation to the Creator—shapes how members of that species understand themselves and behave. As long as we are at home with the Cain narrative, that is, as long as humans think they are primary, humanity will persevere down the current unsustainable pathway.[81]

So the narrative must change. We must retire Takerism's narrative to the museums of the past and recover Leaverism's narrative from the shadows of today. In other words, we must cease raising Cain (in our schools, households, economic enterprises, universities, governments, and cultural institutions) and start raising Abel.[82]

---

81. Even for persons successfully living the Abel way it becomes easy to revert to Cain's way as the default narrative when a crisis comes along. The powers and principalities in the commercial, media, and political world are waiting to pounce on these "opportunities." Such a quick relapse reveals the depth of our enculturation. We have been so thoroughly fashioned by Cain's worldview during recent centuries that we actually see Takerism as the normal thing rather than a recent aberration. But it is in the rough times especially that Abel's values need perseverance. This takes courage in a world where Cain's narrative is dominant and institutionalized and Abel's narrative has been relegated to idealism or museums.

82. Because Cain's ways are easier to accomplish, this is easier said than done. Marketing warfare is always easier than waging relationship, de-evolving into violence is a quicker fix than choosing nonviolent but assertive resistance. Polluting is less complicated than taking responsibility, getting knowledge comes more readily than gaining wisdom, disliking is easier than having compassion, and hoarding is easier than taking what is truly needed and leaving the rest for another time or another creature.

Chapter 13
Is There Hope?

In *Abel Emerging* when I raised this question about hope, I suggested, "Yes, a little." I wanted to express hopefulness, but also to underscore the daunting challenge before our species as we try to reposition our dominant narrative away from Cain/Takerism and invest our time, energy, resources, and economies in pursuit of sustainable patterns of living. Later, my response changed to "Yes, but not in the short-term." Why the shift? Because the megasystems of culture, business, politics, media, and religion currently in place are tooled for the preservation and increase of Takerism for some time to come, and even if Cain decided today to turn things around, it would still require years to retool in a different direction. The old proverb applies: "If it is one hundred miles into the woods, it is one hundred miles out of the woods." So where might we look for leadership?

I don't have a lot of confidence that, in our current economic climate, the necessary leadership from business will emerge. The reason for this opinion is that the business community has generally chosen to adopt an ethic that obliges those in charge to remain ethically neutral. In other words, whether businesses behave as Cain/Takers or Abel/Leavers is not for them to decide, in their view. It is not their responsibility. Rather, it is up to the consumer. If consumers want businesses to be ethical, those consumers will purchase goods and services that are produced, used, and disposed of in an ethical manner. Until consumers put their money where their hearts are so that businesses and stockholders can make money, neither business nor its stockholders have the obligation to be ethical. If consumers want to go down the road of Cain/Takerism, so be it. Then it will be their fault, not the fault of any industry. If consumers choose to go down the road of Abel/Leaverism, they will demonstrate this by purchasing goods and services that reflect this set of values. Since consumers have to date chosen the way of Cain/Takerism, businesses feel obligated to do everything in their power, including engaging in sophisticated and deceptive advertising schemes, to making Cain's way succeed.

Clearly, this perspective is highly problematic, because if business leaders don't lead, then the system is leaderless. And the notion that the market itself—the forces of supply, demand, and investment speculation—should be given the mantle of leadership is also problematic. In reality, the market is capable only of pursuing the goal of "more for less," not in serving ethics or sustainability.[83]

Politicians also offer little hope. Why? Because voters don't generally elect wise politicians. If one happens to slip through,

---

83. There are some private small businesses that are trying to educate the consumer in the direction of sustainability. And some consumers are evaluating the true costs of various products and are supporting them. Can such behavior become the thriving norm? This is the challenge.

we tend not to reelect them. And if they slip through again, we make sure to elect a twenty-to-one battalion of unwise politicians against them. The underlying reason for this is that Cain's voters tend to think in terms of I-centeredness, as individuals, as a nation, and as a species. We are generally focused on ourselves, the small picture, and the short term.

How about the news media? Isn't this industry interested in serving the common good? Unfortunately not. News organizations tend to thrive on human dysfunction. It is fodder for their stories and the hook that insures an audience who will pay attention to their advertising. Do all or even most journalists or companies intentionally choose to act this way? Probably not. But there are forces at work that have an abiding economic interest in sabotaging healthy relationships and responsible living. These forces are the powers and principalities referred to in chapter 9.

I am a campus minister at a major university that has thirty-eight thousand students, so surely I must believe that academia will provide the leadership we crave. Academics are some of the smartest people in the world, after all. Unfortunately, and this is a sweeping generalization, colleges and universities, along with their leaders, are increasingly directly dependent on Takerism's industries and Cain's institutions for their funding. It is very difficult to bite the hand that feeds you. Cain's financial leverage apparatus will always bend academia toward promoting Cain's interests, and will always promote the teaching of students to be successful Cains.

And while I value tremendously what scientists have contributed, many of these fellow citizens have also been untrustworthy. Chemists produce products that pollute not only the soil, water, and air, but also our human bodies. Certain biologists genetically modify our foods with little or no understanding or regard for the long-term consequences. By mixing biological metabolic processes (of plants, fungi, and soil) with industrial metabolic processes (of technology, with its iron, plastics, and oil) copious quantities of non-degradable toxic wastes are being produced every day, filling our landfills. And the horrific nuclear weapons industry could not be built without physicists.

And finally, what about Christians? Does this community offer any hope? Unfortunately church history is filled with instances of Christian duplicity in Cain's worldview, especially in the area of dominionism, as I discussed in chapter 10. The Roman Emperor Constantine (285–337 CE) played a significant role in this movement in the fourth century, effectively replacing an Abel Jesus with a Cain Jesus. After converting to Christianity, he militarized Christianity and helped transfigure the Prince of Peace (one of the names for Jesus) into a champion of conquest. During Constantine's time and since, crosses have been engraved on chariots and missiles, crusader wars have been waged, soldiers have felt they are working for Jesus, and presidents have received military memos encased in Bible verses.[84]

Constantine's imperial assault was not only human-to-human, however. It also functioned in empirelike fashion toward the soil and minerals, oceans and rivers, and flora and fauna. Constantine helped fuse the religion of Jesus' followers to Cain's already-growing assault on God's garden of life. In his book *The Party's Over,* Richard Heinberg describes the deforestation of Europe.[85] In the fourth century CE, lush forests covered nearly 95 percent of Europe. These forested ecosystems (that emerged after the last glacial period receded 12,000 years ago) were central to the lives of the inhabitants in that region, including humans, affecting everything from climate to

---

84. It has been reported and confirmed that former Secretary of Defense Donald Rumsfeld used this method when presenting his policies to President George W. Bush (2001–2009).

85. Richard Heinberg, *The Party's Over,* chapter 2.

poetry, from trade to religion. As one can imagine, sacred stories involving trees and forests developed over the millennia. There were forest legends, religious rites involving mythological creatures and spirits, and even sacrifices, healings, and prayers. There was mystery, there was allure, and there was spirituality.

As a more Cain-like version of Christianity took hold, these forest-related beliefs and rituals came to be labeled "pagan." New Cain-like understandings began to portray indigenous peoples who held these beliefs, as well as the forest itself, as under the spell of darkness and enticement. Their traditions and belief systems were viewed as tainted by ghosts and demons, and as grounded in wild, mythic superstitions. For many, then, it seemed reasonable to conclude that it was the Christian *duty* to cut down trees, clear the forests, push back the chaos, tame nature, and make space and place for the clear, pure light of Christian civilization to break forth across the land. By 1600 CE, Europe had gone from 95 percent forest covering to 20 percent. Surely Abel cut trees as needed. But as Christianity blended with Cain, the exploit of cutting down trees became a holy mission that delivered sacred underpinnings and religious sanction for Cain's already significant war against God's garden.

Have there also been times in history when the Christian community behaved admirably? The answer is yes. For centuries, white-skinned Christians enslaved African people. They were on the side of evil, even as they went to church on

Sunday and praised Cain's version of God and Jesus.[86] But after several centuries of terror, when some of these Christian individuals and groups began to be converted to following Jesus, they became, along with other courageous groups, transformational resources and forces for the eventual demise of slavery in this country. Unfortunately, the nation degenerated into other forms of racism and oppression for another century after Abraham Lincoln's assassination in 1865. But along the way, a portion of white Christians were regularly being converted to truly following Jesus into restored relationship, and, in the end, some, along with African American freedom fighters and others, eventually began to make a significant and positive contribution to American life.[87]

The same is true concerning the equality of women. For far too long the church has been in the anti-God camp. Individual Christians and Church institutions have practiced the exclusion of women from fullness of life and fullness of ministry. There has been inequality under the law, restricted access to various careers, disparate wages, denial of birth control, and voting disenfranchisement. Lately, however, more and more Christian individuals and denominations have begun to be converted to following the risen Christ, and in many cases have become welcomed voices promoting the joys, responsibilities, and benefits to church and society, of equality.

On the issue of lesbian, gay, and transgendered couples and individuals, again, for far too long straight Christians

---

86. Ten U.S. presidents—George Washington, Thomas Jefferson, James Madison, James Monroe, Andrew Jackson, William Henry Harrison, John Tyler, James K. Polk, Zachary Taylor, and Andrew Johnson—men otherwise esteemed as intelligent, well-read, morally upright, and some even Christian, were also predators and perpetrators in a disturbing web of oppression, murder, and the theft of liberty.

87. It is true that among the hundreds of thousands of Abel-Leaver cultures that have existed on Earth's continents, some have practiced various forms of enslavement. And, it is equally true that ours is not the only Cain culture to have this in its history.

have practiced hatefulness and discrimination.[88] The damage inflicted on these neighbors has been enormous. Parents, often under threat and/or encouragement from their church community, have rejected sons and daughters. Qualified employees have suffered discriminatory termination under unjust laws. Committed marriage relationships have been denied or dissolved. For too many persons, years of living well have been lost forever, and the larger culture has been denied the contributions and blessings that come from their well-being. But today, as more heterosexual Christians take the time to become informed, and are slowly becoming converted to following Jesus into restored relationship and understanding, some members of the Christian community are joining others in advocating and practicing fullness of life and fullness of ministry for these neighbors, too.

So what about the issue of sustainability? Where do various Christian churches stand? What is the theology? How does the average Christian behave? Sadly, we have been on the wrong side of this issue, too. As stated earlier, Christians occupy positions of influence in most areas of business, government, industry, education, church, and household. In truth, however, we are doing as much damage as anyone. Are Christians beginning to go with Jesus into restored and respectful relationship with God's beloved world? I have hope, and I see some evidence that this is the case.

What if forgiven Christians were to repent of their war

---

88. It is also true that some closeted gay persons, absorbing society's hatred for them and turning it into self-loathing, have pretended to be straight by being loudly antigay. Even though their unwillingness to embrace who they are often produces a venomous demeanor toward other gay and lesbian persons, they are victims, too.

against God's garden of life and begin following Abel Jesus into respectful relationship with and within the community of life in the Father's household under the permeating reign of God? What if Christians working in mining, agriculture, and forestry, as well as energy development, transportation, manufacturing, finance, telecommunications, education, government, entertainment, journalism, medicine, trade, and the arts, were to let God's gospel and justice affect their careers and home lives? Would it make a difference? Would Christians in the furrows of life be salt, leaven, and light for our species?[89]

Could it be that there would be much hope for our species, and for God's world, if more Christians were Christian, if we retired the dominant Cain version of Christianity and embraced Abel of Nazareth? Might we then influence the curtailing of Cain/Takerism's perilous administration? I don't know the answer to this question, but my inclination is to say yes.[90]

---

89.   Jesus hoped his followers would rise to such an occasion. "You are the salt of the earth" (Matthew 5:13). "God's reign is like yeast that a woman took and mixed in with three measures of flour until all of it was leavened" (Luke 13:21). "You are the light of the world" (Matthew 5:14). The writer of 1 Peter envisions a Christian community that was "called out of darkness into his marvelous light" (2:9).

90.   Cain's theologies have infiltrated the Bible, too. So the criteria for God's truth in the Bible is not whether the Bible says it, but rather whether it is grasped by "Abel's" worldview and theology. Does it cohere with God's primary and secondary missions, or is it part of Cain's diversion down an aberrant pathway?

Chapter 14
Action Steps

Numerous books have been written that outline practical steps to take toward what I am calling Abel/Leaver living. From the annotated bibliography at the back of this book, I call your attention especially to the following;

- *Running on Empty,* by Phillip J. Greene
- *The Party's Over,* by Richard Heinberg
- *Living Green,* by Greg Horn
- *Practical Sustainability,* by Nasrin R. Khalili
- *Cradle to Cradle,* by William McDough and Michael Braungart
- *The Abundant Community,* by John McKnight and Peter Block
- *Design for the Other 90%,* by National Geographic

- *Food Rules,* by Michael Pollan

- *Folks, This Ain't Normal,* by Joel Salatin

These and countless other superb books will help each person, starting today, to make a difference. In our household we compost all compostable waste products to make rich, nutritious soil/fertilizer for our organic garden. We harvest rainwater for outdoor usage, buy locally grown food, and conserve electricity. Instead of pouring toxic chemicals on weeds, we wait until it rains, and then easily pull them up by the roots from the softened soil. There is recycling, keeping technology to a minimum, and skipping ads when watching TV. The truth is, simple ingenuity can have a huge impact locally and beyond.

But having focus momentarily on the practicalities, I again return to the overriding importance of the narrative. When I wake up in the morning, by what narrative will I choose to live my day? From what worldview will I see myself in the world? Will I live the day as though my species has jurisdiction over every acre of the Earth, or will I live it as though the world belongs to the whole community of life, including my species? There is a chasm of difference between these two perspectives, each with enormous and long-term attending consequences. Our species certainly has a right to be here. We are beloved by God, like all other creatures. However, we don't have the right to lord it over others. Nor are we entitled to assume for ourselves the dubious role of benefactor.[91]

Abel's narrative can be broken down into two simple parts, the first of which comes from Daniel Quinn. It is this: vis-à-vis the Creation, "Take what is needed; leave the rest." There will always be discussion and debate over what this actually means in various circumstances. There are different perspectives and legitimate areas of disagreement within the human family, the resolution of which require flexibility and compromise. But the maxim itself is transparent, and the direction clear. We are part of a community larger than ourselves, and wisdom lies in living as though this is true.

The second comes from Daniel Erlander. This says, vis-à-vis my neighbor and the common good, "Live so that all have enough, and none too much." Having too much is deadly to body and spirit, as is having too little. When God sent manna to the Israelites during their forty years of wilderness school, they were instructed to gather what they needed. When they did so, some gathered more and some gathered less. But it was according to their needs and numbers, not their desires. Those who gathered/needed much had nothing over, and those who gathered/needed little had no shortage (see Exodus 16:16–21). The apostle Paul referred to this story in Exodus when, in his letter to the Corinthians, he encouraged the believers to be generous (see 2 Corinthians 8:13–15). Again, the details of

---

91.   In Luke 22:24–27, the writer of Luke understands an important nuance in Jesus' words that neither Matthew 20:25–28 nor Mark 10:42–45 caught. Jesus elevated servanthood as the most worthy form of leadership. At the same time, however, he also delegitimized a social order in which patrons or benefactors played major roles. Benefactors doled out goodies. This fed an illusion of self-importance even as it excused the benefactor from living justly. Such patronage also disempowered the recipients. "The kings of the Gentiles lord it over them; and those in authority over them are called benefactors. But not so with you; rather the greatest among you must become like the youngest, and the leader like one who serves" (verses 25–26). Although Jesus in this instance is referring to human relationships, the same principal underscores the folly of humans presuming to be care-takers/stewards/benefactors of the Earth. See also footnote # 25.

implementation will always require thoughtful discussion and debate. Local circumstances are not the same, and some people have a greater wisdom of connection with neighbors, creation, inner spirit, and God than do others. But as in the first maxim, the meaning is forthright: live so that all have enough, and none too much.

The followers of Jesus are among those who courageously live out such ways. They are the welcomed attendants in God's evolving Tree of Life. They enter into relationship with God, God's garden, Abel, and even Cain. They nonviolently resist and creatively undermine the cancer of Cain at every opportunity, until he repents or becomes benign. They forge a relationship borne in forgiveness and a forgiveness borne in restored relationship.

In summary, a Christian is an expeditionary, that is, one who, in community, is part of a *move*ment and has embarked on an expedition. This life-long adventure consists of three interweaving strands that together fashion a formidable cord (chord). The first strand is the *story/narrative/theology* itself. This book is my attempt to reconsider and recast this story. It explores God's primary mission as it interacts with a scientifically informed appreciation of the evolving story of life, and it explores God's secondary mission, the story of Jesus, as it flows from the context of God's primary mission. I argue that how we think of this story/narrative/message/claim matters.

The second strand has to do with *practices*, that is, the ways by which we rehearse this narrative. For me, the daily and weekly practices of following Jesus involve worship and prayer, wilderness hikes and organic gardening, doing my occupation mindfully, being Ron the barber to homeless men at a local soup kitchen on Monday mornings, reading and writing, cherishing loved ones, monitoring my purchases, conserving resources, recycling, and continuing to learn wisdom from the community of life. Practices shape us over time. They tell us who we are becoming. Each of us might benefit from asking ourselves, "What are my practices, and how are they shaping who I am"?

The third strand of the woven cord has to do with *affections*. Practicing the ways of Abel will in due course affect our affections, our desires of the heart. Over time, a person will lose her or his enthrallment with the titillating charm of Cain, and will no longer find joy in Takerism. Our joy, affection, and desire will begin to lean in another direction. Our interests will grow closer to Abel of Nazareth and his ways, closer to the Abels of the world, closer to the soil, air, water, plants, and animal life, and closer to the Creator. The adventures and challenges of this pathway will become not only our responsibility and wisdom, but also our joy and purpose for living.

Now is the time to join forces, to show resolve as an emblem of hope, and to summon honor as a species. Today, each person can begin to attend watchfully to the precepts of sustainability, and re-establish respectful residence in the community of life. Jesus is on our side and calls us to follow him. The wider community of life is on our side as it yearns for our recovery. So are all the other Abels of this planet. Cain is the smallish one, actually, as is Cain's narrative. Cain is much more diminutive than his noisy chest thumping would suggest. And Cain's narrative is infinitely more diminutive than the life-witness of Abel, the natural magnificence of God's creation, the cross life of Abel of Nazareth, and the "still small voice" of a loving and earnest Creator.

—Ron Rude
www.abel-emerging.com

Appendix A

Biblical Interpretation

My Christian tradition (Evangelical Lutheran Church in America) cherishes the scriptures of our faith. We believe they are the written word of God inspired by God's Holy Spirit speaking through the enfleshed and contextualized lives of its storytellers and authors. Through these written scriptures, which in many cases grew out of earlier and often fluid oral traditions, God speaks to us, calling us to faith and fellowship for radical servant living in God's world—today and eternally after we die.

However, we also note an important distinction between what is known as scripture, and what we call the "message" held within it; between what we call the Bible, and what we call the "living Word" found in the Bible. While these are not to be separated, it is a mistake to make them one. Several images are helpful to consider as we try to appreciate this remarkable collection of books:

- **The manger**: Martin Luther (1483–1546) once used the image of a manger holding the Christ Child as a way to think of the Bible. The manger is the Bible. It holds the Christ. Yes, go to the manger/Bible to meet the living Word/Christ. You will find him revealed there more clearly than in any other writings on Earth. But you will also find other things in the manger, such as wood, straw, and manure. Don't mistake this manger of Christ for the Christ. Don't make the container and God's word one and the same. This will give a distorted (dare I say Taker?) view of life.

- **A cracked pot**: Saint Paul invoked another image: "We have this *treasure* in *earthen vessels*, so that it may be made clear that this extraordinary power belongs to God and does not come from us" (2 Corinthians 4:7, emphasis added). The Bible is the "earthen vessel" (the clay jar, cracked pot), which holds the "treasure" (the living Word, Christ.) The earthen vessel is not the treasure; Christ is. Don't mix them up.

- **Pedestals, and their dangers**: When we humans cherish people or things, we sometimes put them on pedestals. We assume that in doing so, we honor what we've put on the pedestal (a parent, a girlfriend, a president, a child, a pastor, the Virgin Mary, scripture, etc.). Actually, the exact opposite happens. We dishonor them. Placing people on pedestals is a form of control, of putting someone or something on a shelf or in a box. It's a way of keeping someone or something at a safe distance. We idealize them and take away their authenticity, that which makes them real. Christians are impoverished when they put the scriptures, or even Jesus, on a pedestal.

- **A gold-veined rock**: Each week the preacher immerses herself in the text, in life, in study, in the community of faith, in the community of life, and in prayer. The week begins with dead words on paper. The aim is to live those words and to "mine" those words (as one would "mine" rock to find gold) in such a way that the living Word/Christ rises and is encountered. This living Word/Christ is what needs to be preached on Sunday. The living Word does not equal the words on the page, no matter how eloquently, piously, loudly, or theatrically they are orated, any more that the rock is the same as the gold it harbors.

- **The incarnate word:** We humans don't have access to the "pure" word of God in its written form. We only have access to the "incarnate" (enfleshed) word of God in its written form. We only have access to the word of God/treasure as it comes to us through the wonder and messiness of flesh and earthy context (preacher, Bible, sacraments, manger, prayer, earthen vessel, etc.). The good news is that God has made such an enfleshed word sufficient. This, in fact, is the "high" view of scripture, perhaps in a similar way to Jesus' cross life being a life of real "glory." However, the all-too-common rejection of this incarnate word in favor of "purity," which is never attained but all too often claimed, produces only a lowest common denominator and domesticated Christianity in the end. This very common and popular false "Christianity" kills, unlike true Christian faith and living, which gives life.

- **John the Baptist**: The relationship between Jesus and John the Baptizer is instructive. John, like the Bible, came "as a witness to testify to the light. He was not the light, but he came to testify to the light" (John 1:7–8). John, like the Bible, points to Christ. "Here is the Lamb of God who takes away the sin of the world" (John 1:29). And further, John, like the Bible, knows he is not the important one: "He must increase, but I must decrease" (John 3:30). John the Baptizer is very important to the Christian faith. But we obviously miss the point if we "worship" John, or assign divinity to John, or think of John as the way, truth, and life. John's task is to point beyond himself. So it is with scripture.

- **Dogs**: My family had a pet dog named Hershey for thirteen years. If we pointed toward something and said words such as, "Hey, look at that squirrel," or, "See that piece of food on the floor?" or, "Go lay down," Hershey would look at and start licking our pointing finger rather than what the finger was pointing toward. Such is the fundamentalist/literalist approach to scripture. Obsessed with the pointing finger, it misses what it is pointing toward.

Appendix B

Annemarie Russell, singer-songwriter

www.AnneMarieRussell.com

Annemarie Russell is a gifted singer-songwriter who writes from a deep and growing Abel/Christian perspective. I am pleased that she has agreed to share some of her songs with the readers of this book. In the following, she describes her music and songwriting passion, her own honest struggles with faith, and what she finds in her soul that resonates with Abel.

Sometimes the prophets among us aren't those who speak the loudest, but those whose quiet wisdom nudges us with something honest, something true. Ron Rude is one of those prophets, gently asking his readers to reconsider the Christian faith story so that it celebrates the whole creation story and cares for all of Earth's creatures.

I have never considered myself a prophet, but I have had the blessed opportunity to write, record, and perform songs—songs that I hope help my listeners reconsider what it means to be a human being, particularly one who follows Jesus, in light of a broken and complex world. Sometimes my songs are meant to push at people's comfortable notions about the way the world works; and sometimes they are more like gentle caresses, kind words, measures of encouragement.

However listeners experience my music, I have found the medium of song a powerful way to speak out on behalf of those who have no voice and who live in the margins—people living amidst poverty or war, children, and creation's many creatures. As a songwriter, I get to challenge my listeners, asking them to consider a way of life that cares for creation, gives justice to all people, and is full of humility of mind and spirit.

I think my love of music and words was knit into the fabric of my being long before I knew any differently. I was born and raised in the foothills of the Cascade Mountains in Washington State by a family whose members sang everywhere we went. Along with music, I grew up surrounded by a rich Christian faith tradition, but I also found myself continually asking questions that challenged the theology that sometimes felt so dogmatic and oppressive to me. *Why is the church a place from which so many people feel ostracized? What happens when one isn't a "good" Christian? How can we claim to love God and not take care of God's world?* These questions, and many more, filled my thoughts during my early faith development.

I spent my college years at Whitworth University in Spokane, a place that, although rooted in traditional Presbyterian theology, also encouraged me to ask questions and claim Christian faith for myself. It was in coffeehouses during my college years that I first took to the stage with my guitar, writing songs that asked bold questions of faith and life. Since I was never willing to settle for an easy answer, my songs were often filled with deep questions that challenged the status quo.

After college, my husband and I spent a year in inner-city Philadelphia working with Habitat for Humanity. It was in Philly where I finally found the courage to put some of my hardest questions and most controversial thoughts into song. *Sometimes, these days, I'm ashamed to be human, how I long for a sparrow's view*, go the words to a song from my second album *The Finest Hour*. Many of the songs from that project have a distinctly questioning tone, reflecting the heart of a young songwriter for whom traditional answers come up short.

These days I've lost my dreams; long gone are my illusions, life has split me at the seams, and now everything lays crumpled on the floor. Amidst the illustration of an extended metaphor in *Do Without*, also from *The Finest Hour*, I hoped my listeners would hear my intention: to convey that life doesn't have to be the way it's framed by our culture. Each person has choices to make, and on an authentic and honest life path, those choices contribute significantly to how we live out our days.

Some of my songs speak more directly to being Christian in a complicated world, like *Manna*, for example:

> *You knit my soul together in hope*
> *Your stitches are strong and You promise they won't come free*
> *And send me spinning away, away from Your tender embrace*
>
> *You give life, You give breath, You give tears to cry*
> *And a heart to break when my dreams run dry*
> *Let the manna fall down around me like rain*
> *A daily provision from One who will daily sustain*

But even in songs like this one, I still feel tension in my own faith journey. I suppose this is why I resonated so deeply with Ron Rude when we crossed paths at Holden Village during August of 2011. I found he shared many of the same questions I held about traditional Christianity—questions that had left me unsettled and doubtful for almost two decades.

We each have our own calling in life. Ron writes and I sing, but both of us find we cannot remain silent about the things we believe just don't make sense anymore. Quaker writer Parker J. Palmer admonishes his readers to "let your life speak," and both Ron and I are doing our best to use our gifts in ways that speak to others.

So please join Ron Rude in "(Re)considering Christianity." May the words of this wise and gentle man sit with you a while, give you pause, and perhaps change you for the better. And if you find you long for another voice similar to Ron's, I hope you will give a listen to some of my songs. They aren't filled with tidy answers or formulas that make everything better. But I will promise this: you will find a kindred spirit, a companion for this journey, and a friend who asks the same questions that you ask.

Discover the music of Annemarie Russell at:

www.reverbnation.com/annemarierussell
www.annemarierussell.com
or, visit Annemarie Russell on Facebook

Appendix C

"The Widow and the Judge"

A re-worked sermon by Rev. Jen Rude, preached October 17, 2010 at Grace Lutheran Church, Evanston, IL
Luke 18:1–18
Genesis 22:22–31

Jesus told them [the disciples] a parable about the need to pray always and not to lose heart. He said, "In a certain city there was a judge who neither feared God nor had respect for people. In that city there was a woman who kept coming to him and saying, 'Grant me justice against my opponent.' For a while he refused; but later he said to himself, 'Though I have no fear of God and no respect for anyone, yet because this widow keeps bothering me, I will grant her justice, so that she may not wear me out by continually coming.'" And the Lord said, "Listen to what the unjust judge says. And will not God grant justice to his chosen ones who cry to him day and night? Will he delay long in helping them? I tell you, he will quickly grant justice to them. And yet, when the Son of Man comes, will he find faith on earth?" (Luke 18:1–8)

Reaching the top of a mountain, an awe-inspiring storm, falling in love, a sunset reflecting off the water, the laughter of a good friend. When you picture an encounter with God, what does the snapshot look like? Is it one of the things you seek as you come here each Sunday morning?

We wait with anticipation as we hear the word of the Lord today. But today's readings do not give us such picturesque scenes. In the reading from Genesis 22, the encounter looks like a kind of wrestling match that ends in a limp. Our gospel text from Luke 18 presents a courtroom encounter with a corrupt judge and nagging widow. Is this where we will encounter God today?

Or will we end up leaving here today still seeking, still wondering, still wanting to believe, but instead confronted again by the reality that, after being on top of a mountain, we will have to come down with blistered feet, that storms often bring destruction, that people fall out of love, and that once the suns sets, a coldness and darkness descends that can be unnerving.

Where can we find God in these moments, we wonder?

As our hearts sink, we become precisely the audience that Jesus speaks to in Luke's gospel. "Jesus told them a parable about their need to pray always and not to lose heart" which probably means that he was speaking to people who had indeed lost heart. They were people who needed and wanted to experience God—through prayer, through life—but who mostly ended up feeling frustrated and alone, like a pleading widow whose cries for justice fall on unjust ears.

I can't help but connect these feelings with the recent string of gay teen suicides that have occurred over the past few months. We've witnessed young people feeling frustrated and alone, crying out for justice, for someone to listen, but losing heart. They couldn't cry out anymore in the unjust courtroom of hate and bigotry. And so they took their own lives.

Writer and activist Dan Savage and his partner, Terry, deeply saddened and pained by this growing epidemic, launched the "It Gets Better" project on YouTube. It's a powerful campaign. Dan and Terry made a short eight-minute video about their lives, reaching out to gay teens who might feel scared and alone. The premise is this: hang in there, it gets better. It's nothing magic, and not a single word or picture or inspirational quotation makes it all better. Rather, they tell stories of what high school was like for them: the bullying, the name-calling, the isolation. They tell about coming out to their families, and they share beautiful stories about falling in love, starting a family, and what their lives are like now. Speaking directly to gay teens they offer hope: you, too, can have a great life—but you need to hang in there and stay alive. It gets better. They then put a call out to others around the country to make their own "It Gets Better" videos and to post them. The movement is growing. The collective voice of hope is getting louder.

The widow in our story could use a collective voice. She is quite alone, too. The bullies of her day persist in denying her justice. But amazingly, she is the only one in the story who has not lost heart. Something in her sustains her until she is able to wear down even an unjust judge.

So is this what the widow in the courtroom is telling us? Just hang on, keep going, it gets better? Even bullies eventually give up? Even an unjust judge, if bothered enough, will grant justice? That God is far better than an unjust judge, so it gets better; don't lose heart?

Sometimes that is the message we need to hear. Hopefully, this message will keep gay teens alive with glimmers of hope of a future they can't even imagine right now. Hopefully, it will sustain us when we pray and pray and hear only silence for so long.

But is this the extent of the good news? Sorry about the injustice and brutality, but hang in there, keep on keeping on. It gets better. The judge will eventually rule in your favor. Is this what the parable is about?

I was in a courtroom recently with a young person I work with. He's been homeless for a while and is no stranger to being messed with by police officers. One of those encounters landed him in court. In the spectator section of his courtroom were four long wooden benches. (We'd call them pews). An aisle divided them. In that particular courtroom, bulletproof, tinted glass divided spectators from the judge, the accused, and all the lawyers. Microphones allowed spectators to hear what was going on behind those glass walls—court proceedings, paper shuffling, and office talk. But those in the court couldn't hear us spectators. Still, we were expected to keep quiet. If we were not, an armed guard would ask us to be quiet or to leave.

As I was reading about this text for today, one commentator pointed out the ironic nature of this parable. Such a widow, as in our story, would never have been granted access to a judge in her day. She would not have been allowed in the courtroom. Her bothering would have had to take place in the hallway between cases, or in the street on his way to work. Once the judge was in the courtroom, he wouldn't have had to listen to her, since he'd be safe behind his first-century equivalent of bullet-proof glass. Her crying outside would have been quite risky, and an armed guard would have asked her to be quiet or leave.

I was hoping the court case I was involved in would turn out differently than it did. It would have made a great illustration for this sermon. I could have talked about encountering God in that moment when justice was served. The widow had won! But it didn't happen that way. Too often it doesn't happen that way.

So when the moment doesn't come as expected, when the pain and blisters trump the elation of fresh mountain air, how can we encounter God?

Our text says to pray always and not to lose heart. What if

we lived even one day in constant prayer, constant connection with God? How would this change our interactions, our awareness, our attitudes—on a crowded bus, with an angry coworker, with a child throwing a tantrum, or when faced with our own shortcomings?

Praying always, acknowledging that we are encountering God in every cell, every breath, every person. This sounds pretty intense. Maybe a nice God moment would be easier. This constant prayer—this encountering God in every moment—threatens to change us. It threatens to make God an ongoing, all-encompassing, maybe even nagging and at times bothersome presence, with God doing everything God can to finagle a way into our lives . . . which actually makes God sound a whole lot like . . . our widow.

Hmmm . . . What if God is not the judge in this parable, but rather the widow?

The widow is the one who persistently seeks justice, who is often ignored and dismissed, but who doesn't lose heart even when faced with the bulletproof glass around our hearts. The widow is the one who finds a way in. Doesn't this sound like God?

Standing in the courtroom, even in the face of injustice and threats, the widow stays firm. She is not deterred. It reminds me of another person who stands accused later in Luke's gospel, staring a death sentence in the face. He wasn't a widow, but he hung out with them.

This is, in fact, how far God will go to be with us, how far God will go to bring about justice. God will come and live among us. God does come and live among us. Sometimes on mountain tops, in smiles, love, and sunsets. But mostly our God photo collection needs to be expanded. Because our God is not afraid of the blisters, the cries, the heartbreak, the bullies, the unjust courtroom, the cross. And if we seek to encounter God, we are called to go to those places, too. Called to nag and bother for justice. Called to cry out in the face of armed guards demanding our silence. Called to walk in solidarity with those who hunger because we know our voices and our feet are more powerful in 3-D and surround sound. Called to create home out of Sunday school rooms and church basements with families struggling with homelessness. Called to share hope with gay teens that it does get better because we are helping make it better.

So often we want a majestic and powerful God encounter to change us. But what about encountering the widow-God who is all around us? This is the God who shows us how to pray always and to not lose heart. And she is determined. I wouldn't want to mess with her.

Annotated Bibliography

Aldersey-Williams, Hugh. *Periodic Tales: A Cultural History of the Elements, from Arsenic to Zinc*. New York: HarperCollins Publishers, 2011. This text explores the usage and cultural history of the 111 confirmed elements in chemistry's periodic table.

Angier, Natalie. *The Canon: A Whirligig Tour of the Beautiful Basics of Science*. Boston: Houghton Mifflin Company, 2007. With sparkling wit and charm, Angier gives an overview of the essential things to know about science. As a layperson, I found her descriptions especially clear and helpful in the areas of physics, chemistry, evolutionary biology, molecular biology, geology, and astronomy. A Pulitzer Prize winner, Angier writes about biology for the *New York Times*.

Bell, Rob. *Love Wins: A Book about Heaven, Hell, and the Fate of Every Person Who Ever Lived*. San Francisco, CA: HarperOne, 2011. This work gives a fresh view on heaven and hell, as well as the Christian life, from an evangelical.

Borg, Marcus J. *The God We Never Knew: Beyond Dogmatic Religion to a More Authentic Contemporary Faith*. San Francisco,

CA: HarperSanFrancisco, 1997. This is one of Borg's many books that rethink and recast basic doctrines and teachings of historic Christianity.

Braaten, Carl E. *Principles of Lutheran Theology.* Philadelphia: Fortress Press, 1983. Braaten gives a clear and helpful presentation of the main principles of classical Lutheran theology with an ecumenical bent.

Brock, Rita Nakashima, and Rebecca Ann Parker. *Saving Paradise: How Christianity Traded Love of This World for Crucifixion and Empire.* Boston: Beacon Press, 2008. With solid and extensive scholarship, the writers trace the unfortunate move of Christianity from a religion of celebration and promise to one of suffering, judgment, and atonement. This is an excellent resource, although I would use the word *tov* (Hebrew for "good") to describe God's creation rather than "paradise." Also, humans don't need to save or rescue "paradise" (except from humans). We just need to self-regulate.

Brueggemann, Walter. *Journey to the Common Good.* Louisville, KT: Westminster John Knox, 2010. This eminent biblical scholar shows how the Exodus event and the prophetic witness of Jeremiah and Isaiah expose the forces at work against the common good. Immersing ourselves in the immense gifts of God can help us break out of the death grip of dominator systems of fear, anxiety, and greed.

_____. *Theology of the Old Testament: Testimony, Dispute, Advocacy.* Minneapolis, MN: Fortress Press, 1997. The perceptive sixty-page description at the front of the book of key developments in biblical scholarship since Martin Luther to the present are alone worth the price of this eight hundred page tome.

Campbell, Charles L. *The Word Before the Powers: An Ethic of Preaching.* Louisville, KY: Westminster John Knox Press, 2002. Campbell lifts up preaching as an important instrument for exposing and resisting the principalities and powers.

Capra, Fritjof. *From the Parts to the Whole: Systems Thinking in Ecology and Education.* According to Capra, nature is more than a sum of its parts. It is a complex web of systems and relationships. Context and networks replaces hierarchies and analysis.

_____. *The Web of Life: A New Scientific Understanding of Living Systems.* New York: Anchor Books, 1996. In contrast to the mechanistic, human-centered worldviews of Descartes and Newton, Capra describes the world as a myriad of complex and interdependent ecosystems. These living ecosystems are communities of plants, animals, and microorganisms, which have much to teach the species *Homo sapiens* about sustainable living.

Collins, Francis S. *The Language of God: A Scientist Presents Evidence for Belief.* New York: Free Press, 2006. This director of the genome project works to bring science and one form of Christianity together, treating both with reason and reverence.

Eberhart, Christian A. *The Sacrifice of Jesus: Understanding Atonement Biblically.* Minneapolis, MN: Fortress Press, 2011. The author examines the metaphors of sacrifice and atonement, arguing that in both the Old and New Testaments, their significance has more to do with life and ministry than with violence and death.

Eisler, Raine. *The Chalice and the Blade: Our History, Our Future.* San Francisco: Harper, 1988. **www.raineeisler.com**. According to Eisler, the chalice represents life-affirming partnership patterns of human living that were the norm until recently. The blade represents aggressive, death-dealing, hierarchical dominance. Eisler documents the recent arrival of the blade on the human scene and its continuing preference for violence and conquest.

Erlander, Daniel. *Manna and Mercy: A Brief History of God's Unfolding Promise to Mend the Entire Universe.* Minneapolis, MN: Augsburg Fortress Press, 1992. **www.danielerlander.com** . Erlander's book is a superbly creative and insightful overview of the biblical story and message.

Fox, Matthew. *Original Blessing: A Primer in Creation Spirituality.* Santa Fe, NM: Bear & Company, Inc., 1983. Fox explores a creation-centered spiritual tradition as a source of wisdom for people in learning to live responsibly as a species.

Gould, Stephen Jay, ed. *The Book of Life: An Illustrated History of the Evolution of Life on Earth.* New York: W.W. Norton & Company, 2001. Gould's work is an in-depth recap of the story of life on Earth. It includes many photographs.

Greene, Phillip J. *Running on Empty: a Handbook for Understanding and Surviving the Energy Crisis.* 2010. **www.booksurge.com**. Greene's work offers practical explanations of standard and alternative energy resources and how our energy industries work and don't work.

Gustafson, Scott W. *Biblical Amnesia: A Forgotten Story of Redemption, Resistance, and Renewal.* West Conshohocken, PA: Infinity Publishing, 2004. This work is a masterful reexamination of scripture that discovers meanings that popular Christianity often forgets.

_____. *Behind Good and Evil: How to Overcome the Death-dealing Character of Morality.* West Conshokocken, PA: Infinity Publishing, 2009. In this book, Gustafson explores the philosophical, biblical, and theological distinctions between morality and ethics. Morality is death dealing and integral to the dominator systems (Cain) of the world. Ethics is life giving and works for the common good of the whole community of life (Abel).

Haught, John F. *Responses to 101 Questions on God and Evolution.* New York: Paulist Press, 2001. Haught presents a question-and-answer format to explore evolution and the religious implications of Charles Darwin's ideas.

Hayhoe, Katharine, and Andrew Farley. *A Climate for Change: Global Warming Facts for Faith-based Decisions.* New York: FaithWords Hachette Book Group, 2009. The authors give helpful information about climate change and global warming. They also address common questions raised by skeptics. Although the theology is from a more fundamentalist bent, anyone who reads and understands this book will become more informed about climate change.

Heinberg, Richard. *The Party's Over: Oil, War and the Fate of Industrial Societies.* Gabriola Island, BC: New Society Publishers, 2003. This text reviews the history of oil, and how our quest for and usage of it dictates our economic and political policy-making.

Horn, Greg. *Living Green: A Practical Guide to Simple Sustainability.* Topanga, CA: Freedom Press, 2006. The author provides doable ideas for sustainable living at home, work, and play.

Khalili, Nasrin R. *Practical Sustainability: From Grounded Theory to Emerging Strategies.* New York: Palgrave Macmillan, 2010. This book provides helpful guidance for businesses.

Kline, Benjamine. *First Alone the River: A Brief History of the U.S. Environmental Movement.* Lanham, MD: Rowan & Littlefield Publishers, Inc., 2007. The author examines the philosophical foundations and history of learning from, living with, and respecting the natural world.

Kostyal, K.M. *Great Migrations: Official Companion to the National Geographic Channel Global Television Event.* Washington D.C.: National Geographic, 2010. This book presents the migration habits of the Earth's various birds, insects, animals, and sea creatures. It includes many photographs.

Larmer, Brook. "Terra-Cotta Warriors in Color." *National Geographic*. (June 2012): 74–87. This article updates the current exploration of this recent archeological find.

McDough, William, and Michael Braungart. *Cradle to Cradle: Remaking the Way We Make Things*. New York: North Point Press, 2002. The authors offer practical steps on how to innovate within today's economic environment. Part social history, part green business primer, part design manual, the book argues that the reinvention of human industry is not only doable, but is our best hope for a future of sustainable prosperity.

McLaren, Brian D. *A New Kind of Christianity: Ten Questions That Are Transforming the Faith*. New York: HarperOne, 2010. This is McLaren's best book, in my opinion. The questions I appreciate most are: Is God violent? Who is Jesus and why is he important? What do we do about the Church? Can we find a way to address human sexuality without fighting about it? Can we find a better way of viewing the future? How should followers of Jesus relate to people of other religions?

McKnight, John, and Peter Block. *The Abundant Community: Awaking the Power of Families and Neighborhoods*. San Francisco: Berrett-Koehler Pub, Inc., 2010. This book is a helpful description of our culture's devolution from responsible citizen to consumer. In this process, we have inadvertently handed over our family and neighborhood capabilities and responsibilities to detached professionals, corporations, government, technological products, and experts.

Metaxas, Eric. *Bonhoeffer: Pastor, Martyr, Prophet, Spy*. Nashville, TN: Thomas Nelson, 2010. This book explores the life and theology of Dietrich Bonhoeffer, a Lutheran Christian who resisted the Nazis, was imprisoned in a concentration camp, and was tortured and hanged a few short weeks before liberation.

Miles, Sara. *Jesus Freak: Feeding, Healing, Raising the Dead.* San Francisco, CA: Jossey-Bass, 2010. The author shares poignant, humorous, and perceptive stories about building relationships with our neighbors living in the margins of society.

Moore, Charles E. ed. *Provocations: Spiritual Writings of Kierkeg-aard.* Farmington, PA: Plough Publishing House, 2008. This work is a fine and accessible collection of Søren Kierkeg-aard's writings.

National Geographic. *Design for the Other 90%.* New York: Cooper-Hewitt, National Design Museum Smithsonian Institution, 2007. **www.cooperhewitt.org**. This work contains fourteen essays that highlight a wide variety of design innovations addressing the basic needs of the world's poor and margin-alized. Products include a low cost shelter, the LifeStraw personal water purifier, manual irrigation water pump, load-carrying bicycle, ceramic water filters, manual treadle pump, sugarcane charcoal briquette maker, simple furniture, Domed Pit Latrine Slab Kit, inexpensive prosthetic foot, cement block maker, and more. It includes many photographs.

Neubauer, Hendrik, ed. *The Survivors: Tribes Around the World.* Germany: Tandem Verlag GmbH (H.F. Ullmann imprint), 2008. This book presents research about the world's disap-pearing native ethnic groups, from the Hawaiians to the Ainu in Japan, from the Amazon's Zoé to the Xhosa in South Africa. It includes many photographs.

Quinn, Daniel. *Ishmael: An Adventure of the Mind and Spirit.* New York: Bantam Books, 1992. **www.ishmael.org**. This book changed my life by providing a means for rethinking the history of our species, and from there, to reconsidering Christianity.

_____. *The Story of B: An Adventure of the Mind and Spirit*. New York: Bantam Books, 1996. This book helps one further understand the thinking of this remarkable author.

Pollan, Michael. *Food Rules: An Eater's Manual*. New York: The Penguin Press, 2009. The author gives practical wisdom for responsible and healthy eating.

Raheb, Mitri, ed. *The Invention of History: A Century of Interplay between Theology and Politics in Palestine*. Bethlehem, West Bank: Diyar Publisher, 2011. The authors explore various narratives and theologies within Christianity and their helpful and detrimental effects upon the lives of Palestinian Christians living under occupation.

Rhodes, David, ed. *Earth and Word: Classic Sermons on Saving the Planet*. New York: Continuum International Publishing Group Ltd., 2007. This volume includes a wide variety of sermons on sustainability.

Rossing, Barbara. *The Rapture Exposed: The Message of Hope in the Book of Revelation*. Boulder, CO: Westview Press, 2004. This book is an examination of the hucksterism and cynical politics of the End Times movements. It is a reaffirmation of the need to live more responsibly and sustainably in this world.

Rude, Ron. *Abel Emerging: A Reconsideration of the Christian Story for a Sustainable World*. Edina, MN: Beaver's Pond Press, 2010. **www.abel-emerging.com**. My first book laid the narrative and scientific groundwork for what is being further developed in *(Re)considering Christianity*.

Ruse, Michael. *The Evolution—Creation Struggle*. Cambridge, MA: Harvard University Press, 2005. This helpful history of Christian thought, philosophy, and the science of evolution helps provide context for the current debates between some branches of Christianity and science.

Salatin, Joel. *Folks, This Ain't Normal: A Farmer's Advice for Happier, Healthier Hens, Healthier People, and a Better World.* New York: Center Street, 2011. Profiled in the documentary film *Food, Inc.* and Michael Pollan's book *The Omnivore's Dilemma,* this wise family farmer shares practical expertise and philosophical/theological perspectives on wise food production and sustainable living.

Stringer, Curtis, and Peter Andrews. *The Complete World of Human Evolution.* Devon, England: Thames & Hudson, 2005. This work is a study of how scientists search for our ancestors, what the fossil and DNA evidence is, and what are the best interpretations currently of the evidence.

Tattersall, Ian. *Masters of the Planet: The Search for our Human Origins.* New York: Palgrave MacMillan, 2012. The author is curator of the Hall of Human Origins at the American Museum of Natural History in New York. Though I would argue that the title is pretentious, it is nevertheless a brilliant and thorough examination of current palaeoanthropology.

Tutu, Desmond. *No Future Without Forgiveness.* New York: Doubleday, 1999. This is one of my top ten books of all time.

Wink, Walter. *The Powers That Be: Theology for a New Millennium.* New York: Galilee Doubleday, 1998. This is a superb exposition of how the gospel of Jesus is a powerful alternative to the domination systems of the world.

Zimmer, Carl. *A Planet of Viruses.* Chicago: University of Chicago Press, 2011. Viruses are everywhere: in the soil, oceans, even in caves miles underground. Zimmer creatively teaches not only about colds, the flu, HIV, or SARS, but also about the symbiotic relationship between viruses and the development and sustenance of life on Earth.

.